THE
WAY OUT
IS
THROUGH

THE
WAY OUT
IS
THROUGH

Find Light in Your Darkness
Through Our Story of
Marriage Redemption

FRANK AND GAYE GROTE

THE WAY OUT IS THROUGH

Find Light in Your Darkness Through Our Story of Marriage Redemption

Copyright © 2025 Frank Grote and Gaye Grote

All rights reserved.

All scripture quotations in this book are taken from the Holy Bible, New Living Translation (NLT). Copyright © 1996, 2004, 2007, 2013 by Tyndale House Foundation. Used by permission of Tyndale House Publishers, Inc., Carol Stream, Illinois 60188. All rights reserved.

No part of this book may be reproduced in any form or by any electronic or mechanical means including information storage and retrieval systems, without permission in writing from the author. The only exception is by a reviewer, who may quote short excerpts in a review.

ISBN: 979-8-9857599-5-2

Dedication

Our children have graced us with their forgiveness and love. They have been incredible through this process. Gigi and Kevin Calhoun were so excited and happy for us in this project. Scott and Jessica Grote told us how much they wanted our story to be told, knowing it could help others. Matt and Ginger VanderBroek expressed how proud they were of us for persevering on this project. Each of them has poured out their encouragement to us over and over again. We must mention, too, each of our grandkids: Dr. Sutherlin, Kenlin, Tate, Brennan, Tricia, Ella, Livi, JT, Ethan, Gabe, and Karis, as well as our great-grandkids: Adaleigh, and Gracie. Everyone has been so excited for us. Thank you.

Table of Contents

Dedication	v
Foreword	ix
Preface	xi
Chapter One: True Confessions	1
Chapter Two: Gaye's Childhood	9
Chapter Three: Frank's Childhood	19
Chapter Four: Dating	39
Chapter Five: Getting Married	47
Chapter Six: Train Wreck Marriage	55
Chapter Seven: Ugly Truths	69
Chapter Eight: Counselors and Conferences	79
Chapter Nine: Guilt and Shame	91
Chapter Ten: Healing in Paul's Office	97
Chapter Eleven: Deeper	113
Chapter Twelve: Healing	121
Chapter Thirteen: Narcissism	131
Chapter Fourteen: Taking the Wins	141
Chapter Fifteen: Enmeshment	149
Chapter Sixteen: God Speaks	155
Chapter Seventeen: The Way Out Is Through	163
Contact Frank and Gaye	167
Acknowledgments	169

Foreword

In my twenty years of pastoral ministry, I've witnessed countless individuals battling addiction, hurt, and deep-seated pain. Many of these struggles stem from unresolved childhood trauma, with wounds that linger well into adulthood. These wounds can be debilitating, affecting every aspect of a person's life. But I am here to tell you that there is hope. True healing is possible, and it comes through Jesus Christ.

Frank and Gaye Grote are shining examples of the power of Jesus to transform lives. They have dedicated their lives to mentoring those who are broken, guiding them to the feet of Jesus for healing. Their compassion, wisdom, and unwavering faith have made a profound impact on many and have brought light into the darkest of places.

I've seen firsthand the incredible work that Frank and Gaye do. Their approach is rooted in love and the teachings of Christ, providing a safe haven for those seeking solace and recovery. They understand the complexities of trauma and addiction, and they offer not just support but a pathway to true, lasting healing.

The Grotes' ministry is more than just a beacon of hope; it is a lifeline. They walk with individuals through their pain, offering a hand to hold and a heart that listens. Their mentorship is not about quick fixes but about deep, transformative change that only Jesus can bring.

Through prayer, scripture, and personal guidance, they help individuals rebuild their lives on the solid foundation of Christ's love and grace.

In recognizing the tremendous impact of their work, I've opened a pipeline for referrals to their door. I want as many people as possible to experience the healing power of Jesus through the mentorship of Frank and Gaye. If you or someone you know is struggling, I urge you to reach out. The path to healing is not one you need to walk alone.

This book you hold in your hands is a testament to the work God is doing through Frank and Gaye Grote. It is filled with their painful stories of sin, redemption, recovery, and the miraculous power of Christ's love. As you read, I pray you will be encouraged and inspired. Know that no matter how deep your wounds or how heavy your burdens, Jesus is there, ready to heal and restore.

To those already on the path to healing, let this book be a reminder of the progress you've made and the strength you've found in Christ. To those just beginning the journey, may it be a source of hope and a guide to finding the peace and freedom that only Jesus can offer.

Frank and Gaye Grote are a blessing to our community and a powerful force for God's kingdom. Their ministry is a testament to what can happen when we surrender our pain to Jesus and allow His love to transform us. It is my honor to support their work and to encourage others to seek the healing that is available through their mentorship.

PASTOR MATT BEERS
CROSSROADS CHURCH, PEOSTA IOWA

Preface

We wrote this book to share our journey and to let you know there is hope and healing in Jesus Christ, our Lord and Savior. When you put your hope in God and seek Him with all your heart, He takes you on the journey of a lifetime—a journey we never could have imagined when we were lost in pain, shame, and brokenness.

Our story is not easy to tell. It's an ugly story full of sin, abuse, addiction, and the terrible things that were done to us—and yes, the awful things we've done.

Sin.

Abuse.

Addiction.

But this story is about more than our failures; it's about the relentless love of God, who never gave up on us even when we gave up on ourselves.

We grew up hearing Bible stories and learning moral values. Still, we didn't know a real relationship with Jesus was possible. We followed the rules, but our spiritual lives were hollow. Childhood trauma left its mark on both of us—Frank endured chaos and strife at home, responding with rebellion. At the same time, I, Gaye, grew up in an oppressive environment, feeling trapped by strict rules. These wounds shaped our lives in different ways, but both paths led to pain, brokenness, and a marriage torn apart by addiction and adultery.

Everything changed on March 27, 1985, during a desperate fight that became the turning point in our marriage. That crisis forced us to seek help, and for the first time, we began to understand what it meant to fully surrender to God. For Frank, surrender meant letting go of rebellion; for me, it was releasing the oppressive beliefs I had carried for years. It was in that surrender that healing began—not only in our relationship but in the deep personal wounds we each carried from childhood.

God was relentless in teaching us who we are in Him. He used pastors, friends, family, counselors, books, seminars, and video teachings to guide us. One special counselor, Paul Singh, helped us encounter God in a miraculous way, leading to profound healing and forgiveness.

Today, we serve as mentors to others, openly sharing our story—not to dwell on the mess but to point to the transformation that is possible through Jesus. We've decided to share our "dirty laundry" so you can see that no matter how broken your life may seem, there is healing, freedom, and a new beginning through a surrendered relationship with Christ.

We hope our journey inspires you to begin your journey with Jesus, trusting Him to heal your heart and transform your life.

Preface

Then I will sprinkle clean water on you, and you will be clean. Your filth will be washed away, and you will no longer worship idols. And I will give you a new heart, and I will put a new spirit in you. I will take out your stony, stubborn heart and give you a tender, responsive heart. And I will put my Spirit in you so that you will follow my decrees and be careful to obey my regulations.

Ezekiel 36:25–27

CHAPTER ONE

True Confessions

March 27, 1985

Frank was committing adultery. Gaye knew it in her bones but had no proof. Dreary clouds loomed over their modest suburban house, the place they'd once called a happy home in Dubuque, Iowa. Every day, they put on cheerful facades for family and friends, trying to live up to what churchgoing people were expected to be. But behind closed doors, it was a different story. They fought and struggled through a web of lies. Frank led a secret life, and his deception poisoned the very air of their home.

They couldn't go on like this, but without hard evidence, Gaye couldn't stop him. He'd deny it, spin more lies, and continue his charade. He'd perfected the act, smiling through his deceit, leaving his wife suffocating in her suspicions. She needed something concrete, proof that would destroy his mask.

Gaye knew that when Frank traveled to Des Moines for business, he stayed at the Executive Hotel. Determined, she picked up the phone and called the hotel. A pleasant voice answered, "How can I help you?"

Gaye steadied herself, fighting back the tremble in her voice. "Good morning. I'm Frank Grote's wife, and he stays there often."

"Yes, ma'am, how can I assist you?"

"I need to get ahold of him. Can you give me all the phone numbers he's called from his room?"

She heard the sound of papers rustling. "There's only one number." The receptionist provided it to her.

With a pit in her stomach, Gaye hung up and immediately called the phone company. She inquired about the number, bracing herself for what would come. The answer pierced her heart. It was registered to a woman.

The room spun, and the phone felt heavy in her hand. Her fingers shook as she dialed. She took a breath and heard the line connect.

"Hello?" The voice on the other end was unfamiliar.

"Do you know Frank Grote?" she asked.

There was a long, heavy silence. Then, "No, I don't."

"Yes, you do." Gaye's voice tightened. "He's my husband, and I would appreciate it if you would stay away from him."

She hung up before the woman could respond. The phone slipped from her hand. She doubled over. Everything she feared had been true. The confirmation, though expected, hit her like a physical blow.

Her body trembled with exhaustion. She was tired of the lies, of the endless deceit. Tired of pretending everything was fine when, beneath the surface, her world was unraveling. She was done trying to hold it together, knowing that each passing day brought more lies, more betrayal.

She couldn't do it anymore.

Something had to change.

About a week later, Frank arrived home for lunch and slipped into the bedroom, closing the door behind him. With their oldest child away at college and the other two out, the house was empty except for them. She knew what had to be done.

Clenching her fists and willing herself to stay strong, Gaye climbed the stairs, bracing for the confrontation that had been building for weeks. The athletic, forty-one-year-old man who met her gaze on the other side of the door was no stranger—she'd memorized his face and everything about him years ago. But how much did she really know about the man she called her husband?

She squared up to him, every inch of her five-foot-two stature charged with anger and hurt. "Frank, I know you're having an affair."

He sat down on their king-sized bed and looked back at her, his mask of weary irritation firmly in place.

She planted her hands on her hips and leaned forward, refusing to back down. "I found out who the woman is."

Still, he held his silence, eyes narrow.

"Admit it!" she yelled, her voice echoing in the stillness of the room.

"I am not having an affair."

"I know her name," Gaye shot back. "I know where she lives in Des Moines. I called her on the phone and spoke with her."

Frank's expression didn't change, he remained a flat, emotionless wall. He pushed himself up, stepped away from the bed, and turned to stare out the window. His silence felt like a slap, more cutting than any words he could have spoken.

"How dare you lie to me?" Pain surged through every word. She cried, she cursed, she hurled every accusation, every ounce of rage she'd been holding back. The walls seemed to vibrate with her fury.

He kept denying it. Over and over, his lips formed the same lies, the same hollow refusals. His stubborn denial only fueled her fury. She wanted to strike him, to break through that cold exterior and make him feel an ounce of what she was feeling, but she didn't. Instead, she repeated the accusations, louder this time, rattling off her evidence with increasing wrath.

Finally, he let out a long, exasperated breath. "Fine." He threw up his hands in surrender. "You're right. I had an affair with her. But it's over."

A careless admission, a casual acknowledgment, tossed out as if he were conceding a minor point in an argument. He brushed her aside, completely dismissing the gravity of his betrayal.

Gaye had thought his admission would bring relief, but instead, the dam inside her burst, and a wave of torment swept over her, threatening to pull her under. All the pain, the fury, the betrayal she'd been harboring came pouring out. She yelled and screamed, pacing across their carefully appointed bedroom until her legs gave way, and she crumpled into a corner. In light of Frank's admission, their marriage bed felt defiled, the room itself seemed tainted.

His words had made everything real. Painfully, undeniably real. She had suspected it, even known it deep down, but hearing him say it was soul-wrenching. Her heart felt like he had ripped it out and thrown it to the floor, and now, with each word, each halfhearted attempt at placating her, he was stepping on it over and over again.

After a while, Frank stopped talking, shook his head, and crossed his arms. Through a blur of tears, Gaye looked up at him.

His face was hard. "And what about you," he sneered.

"What about me?"

"You get all dolled up and leave the house without a word. I'm home with the kids, and I don't know where you're going, but I know *what* you're doing."

His words hit her like a punch. She froze mid-sob. Her mouth went dry, and her heart hammered against her chest. Her cheeks flushed. Shame washed over her, burning through the anger.

She had been with another man. They'd both been so careful, skilled in their deception. Discreet in finding stolen moments to be alone. Private. Sensual. No one could have known, least of all Frank.

She looked down at her shoes. "You don't know what you're talking about."

"Maybe," he conceded with a shrug. "I haven't done my homework like you. I don't have a name, a place, or a phone number. But I know what you've been up to. Just admit it."

"How dare you?" She shot to her feet. "That's your defense? You just confessed to throwing our marriage in the toilet, and your only response is to accuse me?"

"Maybe." His jaw muscles twitched. "But I'm not wrong."

"Yes, you are." The lie felt bitter on her tongue.

"Admit it," he pressed, his voice hardening.

"You're pathetic," she spat back. They went back and forth, hurling accusations, denials, and insults. His fury rose, mirroring her own, until the room buzzed with the heat of their argument.

How did he know she was lying? It was like he could see through every flimsy denial, every defensive jab. The tables had turned, and now Frank was ramped up, pacing the room, voice booming with rage as he called her every name in the book. She dug in her heels and lashed back with her own arsenal of words, refusing to yield to his onslaught.

Finally, he stopped. "At least I was man enough to admit when I was wrong. Just admit it."

"Fine!" she screamed. "You're right. I had an affair!"

The confession tore through the air like a thunderclap. In the sudden silence, everything changed. All the lies and accusations lay bare between them now, tangled in a mess of pain and betrayal.

A flicker of surprise crossed Frank's face, quickly replaced by a fresh onslaught of harsh words. He threw out a new round of insults, words too cruel to repeat. The room filled again with more shouting, accusations, and anguished sobs as they circled each other, trapped in a storm of rage and grief.

Their voices echoed against the walls of the once-peaceful bedroom, now transformed into a battlefield. Eventually, exhaustion set in. She crumpled to the floor, shoulders sagging under the weight of it all. Frank lay motionless on the bed, eyes hollow, staring at the ceiling.

Neither of them spoke.

The fight had drained them both.

It was the most awful time of their lives.

But in its own twisted way, it was also something else. The truth lay exposed between them now, stripped of all the pretense and lies they had concocted. Frank had admitted what he'd done, and Gaye had acknowledged her own guilt. Their ugly secrets stared back at them, undeniable and painful.

But the admission of those secrets brought freedom.

For the first time in years, Frank and Gaye were facing each other as they truly were. Somehow, it was the most awful, wonderful time.

Gaye glanced at her husband, unsure of what to say next. Despite her deep resentment, she was overwhelmed with a desire to reach out.

I want to tell him I love him, she thought. *I want to say I want our marriage to work.* But the words stayed stuck in her throat. She stared down at her lap instead, wrung out and empty.

Finally, she whispered, "What do we do now?"

The question hung in the air for several minutes, until Frank pushed himself up. He moved to the end of the bed and dropped to his knees.

Resting his elbows on the small bench there, he said quietly, "The only thing I know to do now is to pray."

Gaye blinked, stunned. It took a moment to grasp what he was doing. They'd been life-long churchgoers, but they didn't pray, at least, not together. Not like this. Not in a way that mattered. Sure, they mumbled a few lines over meals or during holiday gatherings, but never in the raw, desperate way he seemed to be attempting now.

His shoulders slumped. His hands shook as he folded them. For a long time, she hesitated, unsure if she should join him. But then, keeping a careful three feet between them, she lowered herself to her knees too.

Frank closed his eyes. "God," his voice strained, "we don't know how to do this. We want to stay together, but we don't know how to move forward. We can't do this without You."

The anger drained from his face, leaving something else behind, something vulnerable and almost childlike. The hatred in his eyes was gone.

"What are you feeling?" she asked softly.

He paused, as if searching for an answer that made sense. "I'm just empty. Confused."

She hugged a pillow to her chest, trying to fill the same emptiness that ached deep inside. A vast, gaping hole had opened in her soul. But now that everything was out in the open, she felt lighter. The lies had weighed them down for so long, poisoning everything. Now, with their sins laid bare, she felt the first glimmer of something new taking root.

"I, umm. I feel hope," she whispered.

Frank stared at her. "What?"

"I feel hope," she repeated. "For the first time in years. I know more truth will come out, and it's going to be awful, but . . . I believe God can work this out."

He shook his head slowly. "While I do actually love you," he said, his voice barely above a whisper, "I don't like you very much right now."

"Yeah." She sat still, absorbing his words. "We've got a long way to go."

That was the biggest fight of their marriage, but it didn't start that day. Their battle had begun long before either of them fell into infidelity. It hadn't started when Frank's eye began to wander during his business trips to Des Moines. Nor had it begun when she found herself lingering longer and longer in the presence of another man.

No, their fight had started decades earlier.

CHAPTER TWO

Gaye's Childhood

As a young girl living in a small duplex in Dubuque, Iowa, Gaye spent most of her time outside running carefree with the neighborhood kids or sprinting down the street to the local ice cream parlor. They stretched on their tiptoes at Harry Kopple's grocery store, peering over the counter at colorful rows of candy jars. Harry would smile down at them, knowing that none had a single penny. Yet, now and then, he reached into one of those jars and handed each girl a piece of candy.

One warm summer morning, Gaye's dad had an unusual sparkle in his eyes. "I'm taking all you kids somewhere special today."

Gaye's brothers perked up immediately. Their father instructed them to pull the seats out of the back of his green 1954 Oldsmobile, clearing space for as many kids as they could fit. Mom packed lunches, and the neighborhood children climbed in, filling every inch of the car. With no seatbelts, they piled on top of each other, chattering excitedly.

"Where are we going?"

Dad just smiled as he guided the car through winding roads into northeast Iowa. Eventually, he pulled into a parking lot nestled among scenic bluffs. A weathered sign read "Spook Cave."

"Who's ready for an adventure?" he called out.

The car doors burst open, and kids tumbled out, laughing and shouting. They lined up, eyes wide with excitement, at the entrance of the cave. Their guide welcomed them as they boarded a flat-bottom boat, ready to carry them into the unknown. The boat slipped down the calm waters of the Bloody Run Creek, and the world narrowed around them. Trees and rocks closed in until, suddenly, the stream flowed into the side of a hill. They entered the shadowy mouth of Spook Cave, and daylight faded behind them.

Total darkness surrounded them. The children squealed, clutching each other as they moved deeper into the cave's belly. The boat drifted through tight passageways and winding tunnels. Stalactites and stalagmites appeared, formed drop by drop over countless years. After what felt like hours, they emerged back into the open air. Light flooded their vision, and the kids erupted in laughter, relief mixing with pure exhilaration.

Gaye's father grinned as they piled back into the car, still buzzing with the thrill of the adventure. On the way home, he pulled into a small ice cream shop. Chatter filled the car as they savored each sweet bite, voices animated, reliving every shadow and echo from the cave.

Gaye's father drove a city bus, and summer evenings drew her to the curb outside the house, eyes fixed on the street, waiting for his bus to round the corner. Sometimes he would stop and let her hop on board, where she'd settle beside him as he steered through his final route around town. The clink of the money changer caught her attention, and she eagerly turned its levers, listening to coins clatter inside.

It was very late by the time the bus was empty, but as they headed back to the bus garage, Dad glanced at her. "Want to steer?"

Her pulse quickened. She slipped onto his lap and wrapped her small hands around the massive wheel. Together then, she and her father guided the bus through the quiet, darkened streets. They cruised into the garage, parked, and climbed the stairs to the driver's lounge, where an old pool table waited under a single overhead light.

"Rack 'em up!" Dad handed her a cue.

They squared off, and the crack of the cue ball echoed through the empty room. Gaye tried her best, laughing as the game stretched on. After their last shot, he said, "Time for a treat."

Back in the family car, Dad drove to Sutter's Bakery, where the glow from inside lit up the dark street. They entered to the smell of fresh dough and warm sugar. Glazed donuts moved along a conveyor belt.

"Grab one," Dad urged.

They savored each bite in the quiet of the bakery. No one else in sight, just the two of them, sharing donuts at dawn.

Sadly, those are Gaye's only happy memories with her dad.

Gaye never saw a brand-new outfit hanging in her closet. Every article of clothing came as a hand-me-down. Her father's limited income didn't stretch far, and money sparked constant fights between her parents. Voices rose, sharp and angry, echoing through the small house. When the shouting turned vicious, and accusations and curses flew, Gaye retreated to her room, heart pounding while her ears strained to catch every word. Fear gripped her, and her thoughts raced. Will they get a divorce? Will they kill each other?

It seemed her parents clashed over everything—how to impress the neighbors, how to raise the kids, and always about money. There was never enough to go around. Special treats seemed like luxuries from another world. Christmas and birthdays rarely brought shiny toys or surprises wrapped in bows. Instead, mostly necessities filled the boxes: school supplies, socks, underwear. Dad rationed every penny, including only a strict allowance for groceries. Mom stretched each dollar, scraping and saving in secret, trying to carve out a little joy for her children.

Once in a while, when enough spare change jingled in the bottom of her purse, Mom dared to splurge. A new Christmas gift here, a small treat there, brought moments of unexpected delight that brightened the otherwise dreary holidays.

But while Gaye and her siblings went without, Dad somehow indulged himself. Their house boasted the first television in the neighborhood, a gleaming testament to his wants. Food never ran short for him, either. He piled his plate high, eating until he was full and then some, as if trying to bury some deep, unspoken pain. His appetite demanded more than just food; it seemed to swallow any extra comfort meant for the family. At five-foot seven inches, he ballooned to 350 pounds, a stark contrast to the lean, disciplined lifestyle he imposed on everyone else.

Despite the family's financial problems, Gaye's mother guarded a secret no one suspected, an investment account she kept hidden from everyone, even her husband. She squirreled away whatever spare change she could manage, silently feeding that account. Not even her closest confidants knew the account existed. Years later, after her mother's death, Gaye, as the executor of her estate, discovered a large, unexpected sum in investments. Her mother's secret nest egg, built over careful decades of saving, stood in stark contrast to the frugal, need-driven life she had always lived. In the grip of an abusive relationship, Gaye's mother had endured years of deprivation and control. Amassed in secrecy, that money had been a quiet rebellion against the hand life had dealt her. Yet, trapped in fear and living as a victim, she never touched it. Gaye proudly used her inheritance for a family vacation.

On Sunday, family life revolved around church. Every week, without exception, the family was seated in the same pew. At Sunday school, Gaye learned all the Bible stories. She could sing every song by heart, and she learned all the rules: don't swear, don't drink, and, of course, obey your parents.

Dad ruled the house with an iron fist and a long list of rules: how to behave, when to come home, and even where to line up the shoes. Any small infraction would trigger whatever punishment suited his mood that day. Sometimes he used his hands; other times he lashed out with sharp, cutting phrases too cruel to repeat. The air in the house buzzed with tension as the children tiptoed through the minefield of their father's unpredictable wrath.

Despite Dad's obsession with control, however, the house itself remained a chaotic mess. Clutter filled the corners, dust gathered in forgotten nooks, and disarray hung over every room. Gaye's mother struggled to keep up, scrubbing and sweeping, but she fought a losing battle against the disorder. The effort always seemed insufficient.

Gaye carved out her own space within the chaos. In her small bedroom, she kept her limited possessions in careful order, each item arranged just so, every corner of the room tidied and straightened. While the rest of the house roiled with clutter and shouting, her room, with its dull, mint-green walls, stood as a fragile sanctuary.

One summer, Dad laid down a new rule: they could play outside but were never to leave the yard. No more visits with the neighbor kids, no stepping beyond the boundary he'd set. Gaye didn't learn until much later that a polio outbreak had struck. Every parent desperately tried to shield their children from the dreaded disease.

Gaye always dreaded doctor visits. The sight of needles made her stomach twist. So, when her mom called her to the car one afternoon, cheerfully promising a shopping trip, Gaye's mood brightened. Maybe they'd stroll downtown and look at the stores. But as they drove past the shops and headed toward the doctor's office, the realization hit. When they parked, her mom grabbed her hand. Gaye jerked back, trying to wrench free. Mom's grip tightened.

They stepped through the door. Screaming and thrashing, Gaye tried to twist away, her cries echoing through the waiting room. Mom dragged her forward, holding her in place while the receptionist checked them in. Gaye's heart pounded as she squirmed and sobbed.

In the treatment room, three nurses closed in, each grabbing an arm or leg. She twisted, desperate to escape, but there was no breaking free. The needle jabbed into her arm—a sharp sting followed by a burning sensation.

Her mother had lied to her. That day, Gaye realized the bitter truth. She couldn't trust her parents. Not anymore.

Mandatory church attendance continued as Gaye grew older. She listened to the sermons and memorized the songs. She believed God was always watching, ready to pounce if she did anything wrong. Any personal failure was reprehensible before God, and sin—especially sex before marriage—was not just wrong; it was shameful. In silent prayer, Gaye promised God that she would not have sex before marriage. She lived with the weight of trying to be good enough and follow every rule she'd been taught. No one ever mentioned grace or that a personal relationship with Jesus was possible.

Gaye spent as much time as possible out of the house. Dad had relaxed the no-leaving-the-yard rule, so she again enjoyed playing with the kids in the neighborhood. She often passed by one neighbor's house. His white hair, wrinkles, and old-man walk were enough to make her want to stay away. But he always approached, oddly friendly. One day, he called her into his yard. No one had ever taught Gaye about healthy boundaries, so she didn't know she could say no. The man proceeded to expose himself, then asked her to touch him. Scared and appalled, Gaye ran away.

In the days to come, he continued chatting in a friendly manner. After a while, he told her he had a secret he wanted to share and invited her into his house. They played for a bit, and he had her sit on his lap.

Then he molested her.

She left thinking she was a bad little girl. She had let that happen. That day, her shame started the lie that turned her into a victim: *She was alone with no one to help.*

Gaye's fight had begun.

She tried to avoid him, but it happened again. Then again.

Eventually, Gaye's mom told her not to go to the neighbor's house ever again. That was the last time it was discussed. No one said a word.

When she was nine, Gaye played at home with the other kids while her parents were out. A family member shoved her into her dad's closet and shut the door. She pulled on the doorknob. Locked. Darkness surrounded her.

Panic struck.

She kicked and shoved at the door, but no one came to help. She screamed until her throat grew hoarse. After what seemed like forever, he finally relented and let her out. She ran to her room and curled into a ball. When her parents came home, Gaye told them what had happened, but there were no consequences for the family member.

Another lie of shame took root: *Nobody cared about her.*

Over the years, Gaye's father grew more unpredictable. The family was always on edge, bracing for what he'd be like when he came home from work. He was frustrated, angry, controlling, manipulative, selfish, nasty, and foul-mouthed. Mom couldn't stand up to the narcissist he'd become. Instead, she enabled him. To compensate, Gaye gave herself a new role as the house peacemaker. She tried everything to please her father, hoping to keep him from raging out of control.

For her tenth birthday, Gaye's mother handed her a box wrapped in simple red paper. Gaye shook it, but nothing inside gave away the surprise. With modest expectations, she tore through the paper and opened the box. Inside lay a brand-new pair of slippers. Gaye stared wide-eyed, hardly able to believe it. New slippers, just for her.

She put them on as though they were the most precious gift in the world, then danced around the living room, her feet warm against the cold linoleum floor. For weeks, those slippers rarely left her feet when she was home.

To Gaye, they were more than just practical. Her mother had saved up money to buy them. They were new. They were hers. She had value!

Every morning, Gaye heard her father in the garage, scooping coal into buckets. The rattling echoed as he walked up the sidewalk and entered the house. She listened as he opened the furnace, tossed the coal in, and grabbed his pole to shove as much as he could into the flames.

One morning, Gaye forgot to put her slippers where they belonged. She stepped through the front door that evening to find her father sitting in the living room, holding her slippers. He glared at her, his eyes filled with anger. Without a word, he grabbed her arm and marched her to the back of the house. He opened the furnace door, and for just a moment, the two of them stood there, staring at the flames. A thick black cloud rolled above the coal, and menacing flames rose.

She gasped.

No. Not her slippers!

But with cold deliberation, her father tossed her precious slippers into the fiery furnace. The one thing that had brought her joy, value, and worth was gone in an instant, reduced to ash.

Gaye ran to her room, collapsed on her bed, and cried. She wailed until her body was exhausted. She hated him.

Maybe in his twisted mind, her father thought he was teaching her a lesson. But the only lesson Gaye learned that day was that he didn't care about her. From that moment on, she wanted nothing to do with him. As much as a child could, she cut him out of her life.

The fight deepened.

Gaye's mother went through the motions of life every day, walking on eggshells. Gaye tried to stay in the shadows.

The other side of the duplex sold to the local church. A pastor and his family moved in. His kids were an improvement from the previous neighbors, so she played with them whenever she could.

After a while, the pastor asked if Gaye would like to go with him on a few errands. Thirsty for positive male attention, she jumped at the opportunity. But then, after completing his errands, the man pulled the car over and stopped. He looked at her.

"Gaye, you're twelve, aren't you?"

"Yeah."

"Well," he said, "when you're twelve, it's time to learn how to kiss."

"What?"

He leaned over and kissed her on the lips. He then proceeded to teach her how to kiss.

She didn't know how to say no.

Eventually, he drove them home. When he pulled into the driveway, she got out and ran to her room, absolutely devastated.

Later, when Gaye told her mom what happened, she brushed it aside.

Gaye's internal fight compounded as the accusatory thoughts reverberated in her head. "You're a dirty little girl. You're a bad little girl."

Gaye was also sexually abused by a family member.

She melted into the shadows. Her fight was in full force.

All men were rotten.

She vowed she would never get married. Never be with a man.

In her senior year of high school, Gaye's brother asked if she would go out with his friend, Wade. Desperately wanting to fit in, she finally agreed. Wade helped her with homework, opened doors, bought gifts, and treated her like a princess. Being around him made her feel special, but it also made her nervous. Wade's kindness unsettled her. She couldn't explain why, but something didn't feel right. It felt foreign, uncomfortable.

After a few weeks, she sat down at her hope chest and wrote Wade a letter. She told him she was sorry, but it wouldn't work between them.

Somehow, she felt safer with the idea of being with a jerk, a man like her father.

It didn't take long before she found someone exactly like him.

CHAPTER THREE

Frank's Childhood

Frank's family lived on Grandview Avenue, a picturesque stretch in Dubuque, Iowa, known for its historic charm, well-kept homes, and manicured lawns. Their modest middle-class home sat just two houses away from the fire station and only two blocks from the prestigious Dubuque Golf and Country Club. Every Sunday, without fail, Frank's mother made sure they dressed in suits and shiny shoes, always looking the part at church. He enjoyed the sermons and took note of the moral code the pastor taught, but at home, he learned a different set of lessons.

His mother, ever focused on her appearance, centered her life on looking presentable for her social circle. The clothes she wore, the places she frequented, and her grooming were all aimed at maintaining an image to impress her friends. Working outside the home was something she considered beneath her. Though they weren't wealthy, Frank's parents joined the Dubuque Golf and Country Club to maintain a certain social standing. Most of their friends spent time there, so they followed suit.

The neighborhood fire station was where the cool guys hung out, so Frank spent as much time there as he could, seeking refuge from the chaos at home. The firefighters welcomed him, always friendly, often commenting on how his mother was well-built and beautiful. It didn't dawn on him until decades later that this desire to escape home carried over into his marriage.

Frank's mother had unusual ideas about health and hygiene. She was convinced that enemas were the cure for nearly every ailment. When he caught a cold, she took him into the bathroom for an enema. If he complained of a headache, the same treatment followed. It was her go-to remedy for just about everything. But there was something unsettling, something that felt oddly sexual about the way it was done. She fondled him.

The touching brought confusion to his young mind. The sensation brought pleasure, but he knew it wasn't right. Every time he got sick, his mother gave him an enema, along with the extra touching. It became routine. A horrible routine. Sometimes, even a simple sneeze warranted a trip to the bathroom for the treatment. He knew it was wrong but still wanted the sensation that came with it.

Starting when Frank was five and continuing for the next five years, his mother did this a couple of times a month. His mind swirled in ways that it shouldn't. When his mom gave the enemas, the negative far outweighed whatever pleasure he felt. Frank made a practice of denying being sick and became adept at covering up every cough and fever.

When Frank was eight years old, he was up in his bedroom one day while his mom was downstairs. Ready to go out and play with his friends, he bounced down the stairs to the landing and looked over the railing. There, in the middle of the living room, was his mother, naked, doing her exercises. They locked eyes. She made no move to cover up. He ran back upstairs, shocked and confused.

After a while, he snuck down the stairs again to watch. He knew she saw him, but she never said a word. If that happens once, it's messed up. When it happens repeatedly, something is seriously wrong. In their house, something was wrong.

Frank saw through the hypocrisy in his mother's life. He understood her thoughts, her actions. As long as she looked good in front of her friends, she was content. That was all that mattered to her. But she was embarrassingly ignorant about many things. As Frank grew older, he began to notice her misguided and even backward political comments—the kind of remarks that would get someone "canceled" today. He didn't know where she picked up her opinions, but whenever she tried to sound sophisticated, it fell flat.

She was a very disturbed woman.

Frank's father was a man of few words. His interests were limited, but duck hunting was his passion. Without the money to buy a boat of their own, Frank and his father regularly traveled forty-five minutes north to Cassville, Wisconsin, usually leaving in the dead of night. There, a commercial fisherman would take them out to a small island on the Mississippi River with their decoys and Frank's dad's gun. Once on the island, Frank and his dad would hunker down, waiting for the sun to rise.

They waited in silence hour after hour, with ducks rarely making an appearance. Frank often grew bored. Whenever he spotted ducks flying over trees and landing in holes far from their hiding spot, he'd sneak off, trying to jump-shoot them. His father, though, remained rooted in place. They never spoke. They didn't talk about school, hobbies, sports, or girls. No words were exchanged between them. As the sun dipped toward the horizon again at the end of the day, the fisherman returned to pick them up, and they would head home. Every weekend during duck season, they hunted in silence, side by side, but never truly together.

A long row of thorny bushes marked the hundred-foot property line between their house and the neighbor's. The bushes looked impressive, but their sharp thorns seemed almost alive, always eager to dig into anyone who got too close. Every spring and fall, leaves piled deep inside the base of those thorn bushes. Their father, always exacting, assigned the task of cleaning out the leaves to Frank and his sister, Gretchen.

With no gloves and no rake, they had to reach in and pull out those leaves, scraping their hands on the thorns as they went. Every leaf that fell meant another scratch or scrape. Hours of hard and painful work would pass before they could call him over for an inspection. But their father never gave affirmation of their work or considered the pain they were in. Instead, he pointed out every leaf they'd missed, finding fault no matter how hard they tried.

When Frank was ten, he often spent time at his buddy's house on Grandview Avenue, just north of Randall Street. They camped out in the backyard, making the most of their evenings. One night, they sat on the front stoop, a Red Ryder BB gun between them.

His friend pointed up the street. "See that streetlight?"

"Yeah," Frank replied.

"I bet you can't hit it."

Frank pumped the gun three times, took aim, and focused. He drew a deep breath and gently squeezed the trigger.

Ping.

"I got it." Frank grinned.

His friend snatched the gun. "My turn."

"You're gonna miss," Frank teased.

His friend pumped the gun, took aim, and fired.

Ping.

They kept at it, shooting the streetlight. Sometimes they missed, but they made contact often enough to keep the game going. After about a dozen hits that night, luck struck.

Frank fired, and the sound of shattering glass echoed as pieces of the streetlight rained down onto the pavement. The racket was unmistakable. Someone in the neighborhood must have seen what they were up to because about half an hour later, a city cop arrived. He gave them both a stern lecture about the dangers of what they had done.

Frank felt terrible.

The officer took him home and told his father the whole story. His dad didn't say much at first, only pointed up the stairs. "Go to your room."

As Frank passed by his dad's bedroom, he spotted the steel brush sitting on top of the dresser—his father's favorite tool for punishment. The eighteen-inch-long steel plate, designed for beating wool winter overcoats, was bound in leather and delivered a punishing blow. Frank sat on his bed, waiting. After some time, his father entered the room, steel brush in hand. "Drop your pants."

Frank obeyed, letting his pants fall to the floor. He turned away and leaned over the bed.

Wham.

The pain shot through him.

Wham.

Tears streamed down his cheeks as the blows kept coming. But after a while, something strange happened. Frank no longer felt the pain and began laughing, mocking his father.

The blows grew harder. *Wham. Wham. Wham.*

When it was finally over, his father walked out without a word.

Frank's mother always had something to accuse him of. More often than not, she was right, he had been the culprit. But one time, she pointed at him, accusing him of something he hadn't done. "Wait until your father comes home," she snapped. "You're gonna get it."

Frank looked at her, frustrated and confused. He knew she was lying, plain as day. He argued his case, but she refused to listen.

When his father finally came home, his mother spun an entire story, twisting the truth to make herself look right. His father's glare landed on Frank.

"I didn't do it! She's lying," Frank interjected, desperate for someone to believe him.

"Go to your room."

"What? You're listening to her?" Frank asked in disbelief.

His father glared at him. Frank knew what was coming.

Up in his room, the blows landed with blistering force. Anger and frustration boiled inside, and when the beating was finished, Frank ran out of the house, desperate to escape. He slipped into his hiding spot between the patio and hedge. Hidden from view, he let loose a string of curses that would make a sailor blush. But the neighbor lady, hanging up her laundry on the other side of the hedge, heard him.

"Frank!" she exclaimed.

Frank felt the weight of her judgment, but the shame ran deeper than just being overheard. He crouched there, alone, wounded both physically and emotionally. Tears streamed down his face as he vowed, "I'm going to make their life as miserable as possible." Then, with a deep sense of finality, "I'm going to live life my own way."

Frank's parents had a routine every Wednesday night of playing bridge with their friends. They often walked to their friend's house, leaving their prized 1951 Chrysler in the driveway. It was a marvel of its time, equipped with a smooth Dynaflow transmission. Frank had spent hours watching his mother enjoy the car's comfortable ride, expertly using the clutch pedal.

One evening, when Frank was eleven, his buddy Ron, who lived just four houses down, had an idea. "Do you think you can drive your mom's car?" Ron asked, a mischievous grin forming on his face.

Frank, always eager for a challenge, replied, "Of course I can."

"You're too short," Ron teased.

"I can reach the pedals," Frank retorted confidently.

"Show me," Ron challenged.

They raced back to Frank's house, hearts pounding with excitement. Both boys slid into the front seat of the Chrysler. Frank stretched out his leg, managing to press the clutch pedal all the way down, but then he couldn't see out of the windshield.

Ron's eyes gleamed. "Let's take it for a drive."

Frank cranked the ignition, and the engine roared to life. They were off.

The boys drove all the way to the end of the street and back, the thrill of it coursing through their veins. Up and down Grandview Avenue, they made several laps, laughing the whole time. They knocked over a few garbage cans along the way. Frank had never felt so alive.

The next week, they were at it again with Ron's dad's car. With a little experience now under their belts, the two boys felt invincible, cruising up and down the best street in town. It became a ritual, a secret adventure for weeks.

One night, just as they were about to embark on another mission, the boys froze. Standing at the end of the driveway were four adults, arms crossed, waiting. His parents. Ron's parents.

Ron's dad was the first to speak. "You're grounded for two weeks. You cannot see each other at all."

Frank's dad simply pointed toward the house. "Wait in your room."

Once in his room, Frank braced himself for the blows. *Wham. Wham.* He laughed. He wasn't going to give his father the satisfaction of seeing him in pain.

If anything, that night only fueled Frank's resolve. His efforts to make his parents as miserable as possible had worked. It was a plan he'd continue to follow.

Frank's sister, Barbara, was six years older and had a rough relationship with their dad. Their arguments often became heated. Once, the tension snapped. Maybe it was about a boy she was dating or maybe it was something else—the reason wasn't clear to Frank. But Dad hit her hard, and when he raised his hand to strike her again, Frank jumped between them.

Barbara didn't stick around long after that. After high school, she packed up and moved to Chicago. She vanished from their lives. Frank asked about her constantly, but both Mom and Dad claimed to have lost track of her. The silence from Barbara lingered like a wound no one knew how to heal.

When Frank was twelve, he sat home alone one evening. Of the three channels available on TV, the only program on was a Billy Graham crusade. He sat still, listening closely as the famous preacher spoke with conviction and clarity.

"God loves you," Graham's voice filled the room. "No matter where you've been or what you've done, He offers you forgiveness through his Son, Jesus Christ."

The words struck Frank deeply. He thought of all the anger, the pain, and the mistakes that had defined his life for so long.

Graham continued. "Jesus said, 'I stand at the door and knock. If anyone hears my voice and opens the door, I will come in.'"

Frank's heart pounded. The preacher's invitation was clear: Come to the cross and give it all to Jesus. At the end of the message, Graham invited viewers to pray. "If you want to accept Christ into your life, pray this prayer with me."

Frank stood, walked over to the TV, and placed his hands on the screen. He bowed his head and repeated the preacher's words. "Lord Jesus, I know I am a sinner. I ask for Your forgiveness. I believe You died for my sins and rose from the dead. I turn from my sins and invite You to come into my heart and life. I want to trust and follow You as my Lord and Savior."

As the words left Frank's mouth, something changed inside him. A wave of peace washed over him as the years of bitterness and anger faded away. Jesus had come into Frank's life.

The next day, he woke up feeling different, feeling something he'd never felt before.

Peace.

He hoped everything would be different.

While he was outside the house, he had a great day. But when he came home and sat down for dinner, his disturbed mother and domineering father brought all the chaos back. He struggled to be good and tried to follow Jesus, but he had no mentor to guide him in understanding right from wrong. His only feedback came in the form of punishment from hypocritical parents whenever he slipped up.

With the constant turmoil at home, it took less than a week before he returned to his vow to make his parents' lives as difficult as he could.

Frank spent plenty of time with a buddy whose dad owned a successful local business. That, of course, meant his parents approved of the friendship. One day, the two boys passed by a house under construction, the partially built walls standing like skeletons among piles of materials. The workers had clocked out for the day, leaving the site quiet and tempting.

The boys couldn't resist.

They climbed around the construction equipment, laughing and playing, turning the unfinished house into their playground. On the side of the lot, they found a bag of cement and a big tub sitting nearby. Frank dumped some water into the tub, threw in some cement, and mixed it up. After a few minutes, they had thick, sloppy concrete at their disposal. They started making concrete snowballs, hurling them all over the walls, floors, and equipment. Nothing was safe from their barrage. The next day, Frank came home from school, and there, sitting in the living room, was a police officer.

His heart sank. He knew the officer wasn't there for a social call.

He sat Frank down and began asking pointed questions about the house under construction. The concrete snowballs had caused real damage.

"This juvenile citation will be on your record at the station," the officer warned. "If you get any more of these, you'll end up at the Eldora Training Center for Boys."

Juvie.

Frank had heard of it. It was for the bad kids, the ones nobody wanted to deal with. They didn't treat kids kindly there. The thought of being sent away terrified him. The officer had scared him straight, at least for the moment.

After the officer left, Frank's dad looked at him, his voice cold and certain. "I'm going to enroll you in Culver's Military Academy."

The words hit Frank like a punch to the gut. He met his father's gaze. "If you do, I'm going to leave just like Barbara did. You'll never see me again."

His dad took a step back. Frank had struck a nerve.

Barbara's disappearance had always bothered their father, even if he didn't talk about it. Her absence hung over him like a shadow. The idea of losing Frank the same way must have been something he couldn't bear. From that moment on, the threat of military school vanished. Dad never mentioned it again.

Frank's dad loved golf and spent time at the country club, keeping up appearances. When he gave Frank and his sisters golf clubs, it made the family look good to their neighbors. He signed them up for lessons, and they learned the basics: how each club had a different role, how to swing correctly, how to keep score, and how to carry oneself on the golf course. Frank took to the lessons eagerly, absorbing every detail. As weeks passed, he began to experience the thrill of hitting a perfect shot. Standing with his feet planted shoulder-width apart, he imagined the ball soaring straight down the fairway before he swung. His backswing was smooth, and the connection between the club and the ball was precise. The ball would glide through the air, landing exactly where it should. Each successful strike brought a sense of euphoria that Frank soon found himself chasing after. He often stayed behind, practicing. He played rounds alone, constantly refining his skills.

Frank signed up for the football team in seventh grade at Washington Junior High. It was a no-cut team, but if there were cuts, Frank would have been the first to go. He was the smallest kid on the field, out of place among his larger, stronger teammates. His coach placed him at safety, probably hoping to keep him safe in the backfield. Frank suited up with cleats, oversized shoulder pads, and a plastic helmet with a single bar across the front.

Drills followed, and after a few weeks, the team suited up for a scrimmage against the ninth graders. They were big, strong, and fast. The running back, Terry Isaacson, was particularly formidable, destined to become an All-American at the Air Force Academy. When Terry easily broke through the defensive line, it was Frank's job to stop him. He got in front of Terry, lowered his stance—and everything went black.

Frank woke up in the locker room. His coach stood over him, shaking his head.

"Frank," he said, "I don't think you're cut out for football."

Frank returned to golf.

Golf became his escape from home life, and the quiet of the course offered a refuge from the chaos. To make money and stay on the course, Frank took a job as a caddy. The caddy yard was a fenced-in area where the older boys swapped stories, smoked, and passed around dirty magazines. One day, an older boy offered Frank a Lucky Strike with a smirk. "Here, Grote, try one."

Frank hesitated, but the eyes of the group were on him. He took the cigarette, lit it, and inhaled. He coughed so hard he thought he might pass out. *This isn't for me*, he thought. But the pressure of the group kept him trying. Within days, he acclimated to smoking.

In high school, Frank entered a city match-play tournament at Bunker Hill. Frank played his best round yet, shooting a remarkable 64, 5 under par. He came home buzzing with excitement.

Gretchen, who'd also competed that day, greeted him with open arms. "Congratulations."

"I just shot the best round of my life," Frank said, still riding the high. "How did you do?"

Gretchen smiled. "Guess."

"Personal best?"

"I won the championship today."

"No way!" He gave her a high five.

But their father remained distant, his mood heavy despite their achievements. Frank, still glowing with pride at dinner that night, tried to lighten the mood. "We've got a pretty good set of golfers here tonight."

His dad shook his head. "What about your second shot on hole three?"

Frank hesitated, recalling the shot into the weeds. "I recovered, still made par on the hole."

"Why did you use your seven iron on the second shot on hole four? Came up short."

Frank sighed. "But—"

"And you completely missed your line on hole eight. Ended up on the wrong side of the fairway."

Frank's joy drained away. He pushed aside his plate as shame overtook him. No matter how well he performed, it was never good enough for his father.

Gretchen tried to intervene. "Dad, take it easy. He played great today."

Their father ignored her, laser-focused on Frank's perceived failures. Beyond the critique of his skills, Frank could feel the sting of the silence surrounding Gretchen's victory as if her accomplishment didn't matter.

All he wanted to hear was, "Great job, Frank." But those words never came. Instead, his father's relentless criticism echoed in his mind, shaping how he viewed himself and his worth in the eyes of both his dad and God. That night framed the way he saw the world, especially his relationship with God. If he couldn't meet his father's impossible standards, how could he be good enough for God? The shame settled in deep.

At fifteen, Frank reached his breaking point. After a particularly harsh argument with his father, his parents left to play bridge. Frank stayed behind, seething. He couldn't take it anymore. Grabbing a piece of paper, he scrawled out a note:

I'm sick and tired of being treated like a baby. I've had it. I'm leaving.

He left it just inside the front door, where they'd have to walk over it to get inside. That night, he caught up with Chris, his eighteen-year-old friend, who was heading to Chicago the next day to start a job with the airlines. Chris was celebrating, and Frank joined in, tagging along with Chris and his buddies as they spent the night out, cutting loose and staying out late.

As the night was winding down, Frank turned to Chris. "I'm going with you. I'm not going home."

Chris paused. "Are you sure you want to do that?"

"Absolutely," Frank replied. "I already left a note at the house. I'm out."

Chris didn't argue. If Frank wanted to come, he could. There'd be a couch for him to crash on while he figured things out.

Frank had no plan. No money. No job prospects. But none of that mattered. He was determined to leave. The idea of escaping the oppressive control of his father was all he could think about. Chicago seemed like a chance for freedom.

They stayed out until two in the morning, and as the adrenaline began to fade, the reality of his situation crept in. No food, no connections in Chicago except for Chris. No idea how long he could stay or what would happen after that.

Finally, he muttered. "Take me home."

Chris dropped him off in front of his dark house.

Frank held onto a sliver of hope. Maybe they hadn't found the letter yet. Maybe they didn't know. He quietly opened the front door. A light clicked on. His father sat in the big red overstuffed chair, facing the door. The look of disgust on his face was unmistakable.

Without a word, his father stood, clenched his fist, and threw a punch. It connected squarely with Frank's jaw, knocking him down, lights out. When he came to, his father stood over him. The dazed fog was still lifting from his mind when his father spoke again.

"Frank, this is my house," he said. "You will follow my rules. If you don't want to, there's the front door. You make a choice."

There was no argument to be made, not now. Frank crawled up the stairs, body aching, mind spinning.

His father never mentioned it again.

Frank spent the summer under the guidance of a renowned golf coach who mentored amateur champions. Frank endured intense technical work, learning to control the club face, refining the smallest details of his game.

By his senior year, Frank earned the coveted first-man spot on the high school golf team. He'd put in the effort and deserved it. After his final competition, Frank began looking at colleges with great golf programs. The University of Arizona stood out, and he convinced his dad to let him pursue golf there.

He packed up his life and hit the road, accompanied by two buddies who had also enrolled. On the first night of their journey, they stopped at a relative's house in Nebraska. Dinner was uneventful, but restless energy took over, and the trio decided to visit a nearby driving range. When they arrived, the man in charge was locking up for the night. They asked if they could hit a small basket of balls before closing. His answer was a firm no.

Unfazed, they returned to the house, grabbed some pillowcases, and headed back to the now-empty range. Under the cover of night, they wandered the grass, picking up golf balls one by one until their pillowcases were filled with at least a hundred balls. They slipped away unnoticed, satisfied with their little heist.

The next day, they drove south and stopped at the Grand Canyon. The evening sun stretched out before them, a vast, awe-inspiring landscape of ancient cliffs and deep gorges. Frank couldn't resist. He grabbed his driver and the bulging sack of balls. Standing at the edge of the canyon, he teed up the first ball. The club connected with a sharp, clean sound. The ball sailed through the air, arcing over the canyon before ricocheting off the rocky walls and disappearing into the depths.

He grinned.

Another ball teed up, another effortless swing. Frank watched, mesmerized, as it flew even further. He tried to hit it hard enough that he couldn't see it land. Soon, his buddies joined in. The quiet of the Grand Canyon was interrupted by the thwack of golf clubs and the cheering of an impromptu crowd that had gathered. Strangers watched and cheered them on, captivated by the sight of golf balls vanishing into the abyss. Thankfully, no park rangers showed up to ruin their fun. Finally tiring of the game, they climbed back into the car with broad smiles and laughter. The rest of the trip passed in a blur of jokes and boasts about who had hit the longest drive into the canyon. Frank couldn't help but wonder how many people might stumble upon those golf balls in the years to come, deep in the cracks and crevices of the Grand Canyon.

At the University of Arizona, Frank settled into a typical college routine, signing up for classes, fulfilling the ROTC requirement, and joining the golf team. He attended every practice, eager to prove himself. Unfortunately, first-year students rarely got a chance to play in tournaments, which left him restless. He and a group of like-minded students founded the Alpha Epsilon fraternity. The others in the group were sharp, quick-witted, and at ease around women, while Frank often found himself feeling out of place, unsure why he was even there.

They threw bonfire parties in the desert, inviting as many girls as they could. Frank drank to fit in, and before long, weekends blurred into drunken nights. It became a habit that felt increasingly normal. He noticed some of his fraternity brothers spiking drinks with vodka and other hard liquor at the parties. That didn't sit right with him. He wanted to know what he was drinking, so he stuck with beer. He was in control of not being in control.

Despite his drinking and social life, Frank focused on his classes and aimed for a business degree. After about a month on campus, he received a note from the dean of the business school, requesting a meeting. Sitting across from the dean in his office, Frank answered a series of polite questions about his classes, living situation, and social life. Then the dean leaned forward and said, "Frank, do me a favor."

"What's that?" Frank asked.

"Call your father and let him know you're okay. He's been in touch, wondering if you're still alive. We don't babysit our students here. That's your job."

Frank returned to his dorm and called home. He assured his dad that everything was fine and there was no trouble. The call was short and businesslike.

Frank was doing well enough academically, pulling A's and B's in his regular classes. But at the end of the second semester, he received an order from the commandant of the ROTC program demanding his presence in the office. Frank suited up in his ROTC uniform and knocked on the door.

The commandant looked over his file. "Your grades aren't too bad," he said.

"No, sir," Frank replied.

"But I understand you're not attending ROTC class."

"No, sir. I'm not."

"Would you mind explaining why?"

"Sir, the ROTC program is a waste of taxpayer money," Frank said bluntly. He launched into a detailed account of the program's inefficiencies and absurdities, railing against government waste.

The commandant said, "I can't agree with you, but I won't disagree either."

"Thank you, sir."

"But I'm going to have to flunk you."

"Yes, sir. I understand."

"Dismissed."

As Frank reached for the door, the commandant called out. "Grote!"

Frank turned. "Yes, sir?"

"You don't give a damn, do you?"

"No, sir. I don't."

Frank left the office without a second thought, heading to the golf course to work on his swing. He wasn't expelled, but there'd be work ahead to dig himself out of the mess he'd made.

A week later, Frank was back home in Dubuque for the summer. He greeted his mother, and then Gretchen peppered him with questions during a long walk. That evening, however, something felt off in the house. The air was heavy, as though something was about to break.

Frank's dad sat at the dinner table, glaring at him. "Your grades came today."

Frank nodded.

"You've got a B average."

"Thanks."

"But any dumb SOB can pass ROTC."

Frank laughed.

His father remained stone-faced. "Tomorrow, you're heading to the University of Dubuque to sign up for classes."

Frank's mouth dropped open. He hadn't expected this. He had miscalculated his father's reaction entirely. The next day, Frank enrolled at the University of Dubuque (UD). His experience with the golf team in Arizona left a sour taste in his mouth, so he didn't even bother joining the UD team. He rejoined old friends from town instead and went looking for excitement. After countless parties, his new girlfriend told him she was pregnant. Reluctantly, he proposed to her because that was the only socially acceptable option. Then, through the rumor mill, he discovered she'd been lying and wasn't pregnant, so he planned to break it off.

Then he set his eyes on a cute coed.

CHAPTER FOUR

Dating

Gaye had graduated from high school, but she wasn't ready to handle a job and she knew it. Her father gave her two options: work full-time or go to school. She turned to the University of Dubuque despite her shaky high school grades. To her relief, they accepted her on probation, allowing her to start that fall. Orientation came with an odd tradition: a blue and white baseball cap with a tiny bill. They insisted she wear it at all times. She donned the beanie reluctantly, quickly realizing it marked her as a freshman. It wasn't long before older students called out snide remarks as she passed.

One morning she was seated in chapel, her Bible open, following the chaplain's words. As the sermon carried on, however, a strange, constricting feeling closed around her chest. She couldn't breathe. Darkness crept in at the edges of her vision, pulling her back to a place she thought she'd left behind—a tight, airless space, like the closet she'd been locked in as a child. She was trapped. Alone. The chaplain's voice became a distant echo, lost in the storm swelling within. Her struggle was not just physical; it was a war of emotions and fears.

Overwhelming … debilitating … panic.

Her heart thundered against her ribcage, sweat gathered on her skin, and her limbs shook. Fear took hold, its grip relentless. Her chest burned, demanding escape. She stood abruptly, then made her way out as steadily as she could, trying to appear calm. Out in the fresh air, she paced until her breathing slowed and her mind cleared, but the terror lingered. Alone in her confusion, she didn't share it with anyone.

Weeks later, another attack struck, this time in a classroom. The air seemed to disappear, the walls pressed in.

Once again, she fled the room. She sucked in deep breaths, telling herself to calm down. What was going on? Was she dying?

From then on, she sat by the door in every class, ready to escape if needed. The panic came like clockwork every few weeks, closing around her like a net. She held her fear in silence, but her world shrank a little more with every attack. Even the sky seemed threatening, pressing down in ways she couldn't explain, but she was always alone in her terror.

She'd made the grades to return as a sophomore, finally free of that humiliating freshman beanie but with a need for affirmation. She clung to her promise to God to wait until marriage to have sex. Still, she craved attention, feeling drawn by the allure of being noticed. Other girls had prom dates and homecoming dances. She didn't, but she dressed to stand out, bleaching her hair blond. Until now, any male attention that had come her way had been either harsh and critical or abusive. Catcalls from the guys on campus were thrilling.

Walking down a staircase in front of Steffens Hall, she noticed a handsome young man looking her way with a smile. She'd seen him before, knew his name was Frank, but she took little notice because rumors circulated that he was engaged. As the days passed, Frank kept smiling at her.

The university hosted an annual ski party over winter break at Chestnut Mountain in Galena, Illinois. Gaye went with friends and spotted Frank there. They made small talk, which felt easy. Near the end of the day, Frank turned to her, a casual smile on his face.

"Would it be okay if I gave you a ride home?"

Without hesitation, she replied, "No, I'm not going home with you. You're engaged."

He chuckled. "I am, but I won't be next week."

A friend drove her home. She pushed Frank out of her mind for the rest of the school year. But the following summer, out of the blue, the phone rang.

"Hello?"

"This is Frank Grote. Want to go for a ride with me?"

She said nothing.

"By the way," he added, "I'm not engaged anymore."

She hesitated but wasn't occupied that evening. "Sure."

He took her to Eagle Point Park, a serene, scenic area in Dubuque along the bluffs, famous for its sweeping Mississippi River views and inviting pathways. As the sun dipped low, they strolled through the park, warmed by the glow of streetlights. He asked about her studies and plans. His questions put her at ease, and she began to relax, enjoying the evening.

Their conversation drifted to golf and tales from his fire station buddies. Frank's stories carried a contagious energy, and Gaye couldn't help but laugh as he shared one funny tale after another. But as they talked, the park lights suddenly turned off, leaving them in complete and unexpected darkness.

You son of a gun, she thought. *You planned this whole thing to get me here in the dark.*

But Frank merely led her back to his car and took her home without a hint of anything more. Later, he'd admit he was just as nervous as she'd been.

A week later, Frank invited her to watch him compete in the country club golf championship. She'd never been on a golf course, let alone in a place as elite as a country club. Coming from a modest background, she worried about how the other guests would see her. What if she spoke out of turn or wandered somewhere off-limits? She wore her best dress, determined to blend in, and walked to the golf course.

When she arrived, Frank was warming up, surrounded by other well-dressed men confidently swinging their clubs. She felt lost. An older woman noticed her hesitancy and took her under her wing. The woman guided her around the course, explaining the game, pointing out who was who, and narrating each stage of the event. Frank went on to win the championship. The woman nudged her. "Go give him a kiss."

Gaye's feelings of inadequacy and discomfort were palpable. "I'm not kissing him. I hardly know him."

Instead, she approached him and politely said, "Congratulations." The significance of his win eluded her, but she noticed the pride in his eyes.

For their next date, Frank took her to his sister's wedding. Surrounded by elegant clothes, fragrant flowers, and cheerful chatter, she marveled at the appearance of joy in the room. Guests rose one after another to give heartfelt speeches about the couple, celebrating their commitment and blessing their new life together. Frank moved comfortably through the crowd, chatting and laughing, while she stayed in the background, feeling very out of place.

As they continued dating, Gaye introduced Frank to her family. He was comfortable and gregarious in their home. As she watched him interact with her parents, she started to fall in love. A few weeks later, Frank asked her to go steady.

They were a couple.

Gaye was on cloud nine. She had a guy, a status symbol. All those times she'd believed she'd never have a man were over. For the first time in her life, she felt special, validated. Frank was *her man*.

Frank set up a dinner and movie night, promising to pick her up at six. She dressed early, eager to see him, and sat by the window. But six o'clock came and went, and he didn't show. She waited, holding onto hope, but after an hour, she made a sandwich, retreated to her room, and gave up. The next day, he called as if nothing had happened.

"Hey, can we get together soon?"

"Where were you?" Anger tightened her voice.

"Oh, I just got caught up playing cards with the guys at the fire station and lost track of time. I'll make it up to you."

"I waited for hours." Her disappointment hardened.

"I'm so sorry. Let's go out tonight. We'll grab a bite and catch that movie."

They had a good evening together, but when he didn't show up again a few weeks later, Gaye drove to the fire station. There he was, playing cards with his friends. She approached with her hands on her hips. They left together and drove to the Tick Tock Bar in East Dubuque, where they danced the evening away.

As the dates continued, Frank started pressuring her to have sex. She refused, explaining the vow she'd made to God to wait until marriage. But he didn't let up, coaxing and pushing, leaving her torn and vulnerable. Over the months, his persistence began to wear her down. She feared he might be the only man who'd ever want her. Finally, despite her own conviction, she relented and abandoned her promise.

When she woke the next morning, an overwhelming shame weighed upon her, settling in her heart like a dark cloud. She cried, consumed by regret. Appetite fled. Sleep eluded her. She found herself desperate for refuge.

Losing her virginity created a seismic shift, an emotional and spiritual wound. Frank had taken the one sacred thing she believed was hers alone to give. Despite having no relationship with Jesus, Gaye felt the need to go to church. She needed to return to God, hoping He might heal the pain that clawed at her.

She withdrew from Frank and couldn't look him in the eye. Within a week, Frank showed interest in another girl who was in town for a golf tournament. His disregard confirmed the belief Gaye feared all along—no one would ever truly care for her.

Her shame deepened. A devastating ache left her struggling to pick up the pieces. Gaye dropped out of college and took a job as a medical assistant at an ob-gyn office.

At the end of the summer, Frank called Gaye again. He explained the other girl was out of the picture, and he told Gaye he still loved her. Just like that, he wanted her back. Helpless and victimized, she let him back in. Her life was an open book. She told Frank she loved him and confirmed that she hadn't been with anyone else.

A few months passed, and Gaye became concerned that she might be pregnant. With no home pregnancy tests available back then, she took the medical technologist at her office a urine sample, saying it was "for a friend."

A week later, he caught her in the hallway. "You can tell your friend she is, in fact, pregnant."

Shame flooded her being. The thought of raising a child paralyzed her.

That evening, Frank pulled up outside the clinic to take her home. She walked to his car, feeling the weight of her burden with every step. She shut the door behind her and said, "Hi, Dad."

He glanced at her. "What's going on?"

She crossed her arms over her belly and told him the news.

They sat in the car, silence pressing down, neither one knowing what to say. Finally, he asked, "Now what?"

CHAPTER FIVE

Getting Married

Frank broke the silence, voice low and somber. "We need to talk with somebody."

Gaye met his eyes, voice barely a whisper. "The only person I trust is my pastor."

Without another word, Frank drove to the church. Inside, the minister listened quietly, and after a moment, he folded his hands, looking from one to the other. "I don't condone what you two have done," he said gently, "but, Frank, do you love Gaye?"

"Yes."

The minister turned to her. "Gaye, do you love Frank?"

"Yes."

"Then we're going to make this right. You're going to get married." He spoke with the authority of decision, and the weight of it settled on both of them. They set the date for March 12, 1966.

Frank shifted his gaze to her, voice hesitant. "I guess we need to tell our parents."

Her mouth dried up. "What are we going to say?"

Frank looked down. "This isn't going to go well."

The minister gave them a steady nod. "Telling news like this is hard. It's better to get it over with tonight. Just rip off the Band-Aid."

Moments later, they were driving to Frank's parents' house. Frank parked, then walked around and opened her door. She hesitated before following him up the front steps. Frank's father sat watching golf, his expression neutral as they entered.

"Is Mom home?" Frank asked.

His dad nodded toward the stairs.

Frank called his mother down. They gathered in the living room, his parents eyeing them with suspicion.

Frank cleared his throat. "We've got something to tell you."

His parents exchanged glances.

"Gaye is going to have a baby."

A brief silence hung before his mother reacted. "What are my friends gonna think?"

Frank said, "I'm sorry, Mom."

She pushed forward, her finger pointing accusingly at Gaye, an expression of fury and disdain contorting her face. "You got my son pregnant."

Gaye took a step back, stunned.

A torrent of vicious words erupted from Frank's mother, each one cutting deep.

Gaye continued stepping back until she was pressed against the wall.

Frank's father watched from the couch, silent and unreadable. His wife continued her bizarre tirade.

Frank's voice rose above the storm. "Mom, settle down. I'm sorry. I know this isn't what you wanted."

"*Not* what I *wanted*?" Her eyes flashed with indignation as she repeated his words. This baby is out of wedlock. We'll not have anything to do with this child." Her voice filled the room, each sentence more scornful than the last.

Gaye stood frozen, the barrage of words leaving her breathless. Frank took her hand and gently pulled her toward the door. "We're sorry you feel that way."

Outside, they stumbled to the car, brushing away tears.

Gaye exhaled. "That woman is evil."

Frank held her hand. "I know."

"I've never felt hatred from anyone like that."

"I'm sorry. My mom has a way about her. She wanted me to marry a doctor's daughter or a lawyer's daughter."

Gaye looked away. "I'm not good enough?"

He ran a hand down his face. "She's just an angry woman."

Gaye sank into her seat, feeling hollow and worthless. "What's wrong with her?"

Frank exhaled. "She went through a lot. She was abused as a kid and cut off from her family for marrying my dad. When her father was dying, they wouldn't even let her in the house to say goodbye."

She shook her head. "That's no excuse. No one should treat anyone like that."

"I know," he replied. "I'm sorry."

The engine of Frank's Buick grumbled as he drove them toward her parent's house for a second round of difficult news. They parked in the alley and slipped quietly in through the back door. The house was still. Gaye moved to the window, watching the street. Her mother's shift at Finley Hospital should be over soon; she'd be home any minute.

Just then, her mother appeared on the sidewalk, her face flushed, jaw set. The door swung open, and she stepped inside.

"Oh, you're here," she said. "I know all about it."

"How?" Gaye stammered.

"The pastor came by the hospital." Her voice had a hard edge. "He congratulated me on a wonderful grandchild." She crossed her arms and stared them down, her gaze sharp.

Frank and Gaye eased onto the worn sofa. Gaye's apologies came tumbling out, while Frank's gaze remained locked on the floor.

Finally, her mother's shoulders relaxed, and her voice softened. "I'll support you two."

Relief washed over Gaye. She swallowed back tears. Frank muttered a brief response and disappeared into the bathroom. Gaye's mother squeezed her hands, then pulled out a tissue.

When Gaye's dad came home, they repeated the process. He took some time to come around, but eventually he said the same: "We'll support you."

Like any little girl, Gaye had dreamed of her wedding—colors and flowers chosen carefully, the music swelling as she walked down the aisle beside her father. But now, with the date set, she knew it wouldn't be anything close to the day she'd once imagined. Her thoughts drifted to the memory of Frank's sister's wedding, full of smiles and laughter, family members gathered in joy. Her wedding would be so different.

Meanwhile, in the world outside of Dubuque, the chaos in Vietnam was in full swing. Every evening, Walter Cronkite's solemn voice narrated while pixelated scenes flashed on the screen. The draft loomed over every young man in America, a shadow growing ever darker since its enactment in 1964. Frank watched it all from his couch—young men leaving for duty strong, hopeful, and healthy, returning with scars, missing limbs, or not at all.

Every day, he walked to the mailbox, holding his breath. For a long while, it didn't come, but then one day, the letter was there. Frank's number was up, and he was summoned to Des Moines. On a cold morning, he joined a line of young men. They measured him at 5 foot, 9 inches, 128 pounds. A doctor checked his vitals and looked him over.

"Fit for duty," he declared. Frank's future seemed certain.

Fear gripped Gaye's heart as she counted down the days for when Frank was scheduled to report to the office. Helpless against the relentless march of time, they packed and prepared, but nothing anyone could say would really soften the blow.

The day came, and Frank reported for duty. A clerk called him back into an interview room and flipped through his file with little fanfare.

"You're getting married?" the man asked, glancing up from the paperwork.

"Yes, sir."

His eyes dropped back to the page. "She's pregnant?"

Frank nodded.

The clerk reached for a stamp and slammed it onto the file.

"You're dismissed," he said, his voice final. "You're not going to Vietnam."

Frank left the office, heart racing, filled with disbelief and awe. God had provided His divine protection.

When Gaye heard the news, she breathed a sigh of relief. Then she headed out, alone, in search for a wedding dress. She scanned the racks at Roshek's Department Store, where a pink brocade suit caught her eye, neat and sweet. She turned it over, picturing herself on her wedding day. The suit included a tiny bow for her hair and a delicate veil attached to the back. She slipped it on, smoothing the fabric and eyeing herself in the mirror. In satin heels and pearl earrings, she thought of how her body would grow with her baby, her hundred-pound frame slowly filling with new life.

Gretchen appointed herself the wedding planner. With only a few weeks to pull it together, Gaye got out of Gretchen's way and let her do her thing. She arranged a small reception at the Dodge House Restaurant, picked out flowers, decorations, and cake.

On the day of the wedding, the group gathered at the church under a dark, rainy sky. Gaye's brother Ralph busied himself in the parking lot, decorating the family's metallic blue 1964 Buick with cans and streamers. He was the only one in a cheerful mood. Frank's parents cried bitter tears through the entire ceremony and were red-eyed in every photo. Gaye's parents managed to keep their emotions contained, quietly accepting the inevitable.

Frank stood beside Gaye, but the hangover he nursed from a wild night before made him look green. After the brief ceremony and reception, they changed clothes, slipped into the decorated car, and drove across the Mississippi River.

Somehow, as the newly married couple crossed the bridge, the day's tension floated away. They were free from the oppression, away from all the condescending looks and comments. Finally, they could enjoy a moment all their own. Euphoria.

When they arrived at the Madison Holiday Inn, they flopped down together on the bed. Gaye noticed a slot on the side for quarters. Grinning, she popped in a coin and hit the button. The bed shook wildly. Gaye doubled over laughing until Frank turned green again.

By evening, he'd recovered. They enjoyed a peaceful dinner, their first night together as husband and wife.

As they packed up the following day, Frank slipped an ashtray marked with the Holiday Inn logo into their bag.

Gaye's eyes widened. "What are you doing?"

"Keeping a souvenir."

"They'll catch us!"

Frank shrugged. "You worry too much." He closed the bag, grinning, and they headed out the door.

Back in Dubuque, since Frank was still enrolled at UD, they settled into married student housing. Frank stashed the ashtray, his keepsake of that night, in a drawer somewhere. In time, it disappeared. Cottage number eight became their new home, a cozy, five-hundred-square-foot space. The tiny kitchen, half bath, and small living area formed the full extent of their little world. Gaye dressed it up the best she could with striped orange and cream curtains in the kitchen, matching dishes, and a couple of pillows on the sofa that doubled as their bed.

When baby Gigi arrived, Gaye quit her job and stayed home. She fashioned a nursery by hanging a curtain between two closets at the end of the room and decorating it in the same orange and cream theme. The young couple shuffled pillows, blankets, and baby toys out of sight whenever friends showed up. It was chaos but pure joy.

CHAPTER SIX

Train Wreck Marriage

As a young married couple, Frank and Gaye kept up the appearance of a young Christian family, sitting in the pews every Sunday. With both sets of parents nearby, they had no shortage of babysitters. On Friday nights, they dropped Gigi off with a grandparent and headed out. Eight guys and their girlfriends or wives became their central circle of friends. They spent Friday and Saturday nights together, forging routines that solidified as girlfriends transformed into wives.

Frank was a happy drunk. He'd tell jokes and spin the same stories, reliving his glory days. The women talked about their kids and often devolved into husband bashing. Later in the night, Frank and Gaye hit the bars to catch their favorite bands. Frank sang along, sometimes even persuading the band to let him take the stage. Saturday evenings followed the same script: rinse and repeat.

As months wore on, the bars filled with familiar faces who expected Frank and Gaye Grote to show up. One establishment even had bar stools with their names on them. Gaye didn't enjoy the long raucous nights and longed to be home, but not knowing she could say no, she stayed by Frank's side, even at local strip clubs.

Their weekend escapades necessitated plenty of recovery time. When Frank was home, he slept. All Gaye wanted was for him to be home with her and Gigi.

Striving to be the "good wife," Gaye cooked, did countless loads of laundry, and kept a pristine home. Alone most of the day, she fed, changed, and cared for their precious child. Many afternoons, she took Gigi to the park or playground, hoping to escape the suffocating silence of their home. But even amid laughter and sunlight, tears spilled down her cheeks. She longed to return to her mother's house, where love and care felt more tangible.

Eventually Gaye began refusing to go out with Frank, and when she did, he simply shrugged and ventured out without her. She went to her mother's place, searching for a semblance of comfort. There, the weight of loneliness lifted, but in her own home, it loomed larger with every passing day. Gaye recognized the weight of the long, grueling haul ahead. She was trapped.

Frank lived life on his own terms. He played golf whenever the mood struck and hunted or fished as he pleased. Gaye and Gigi weren't much more than an afterthought, a distant consideration in the whirlwind of his life.

While Gaye didn't confront him directly about his neglect, she complained when he missed meals and announced that Gigi took her first steps without him. He didn't seem to care. He ignored or didn't recognize her coded language and passive-aggressive hints. She never did square up to him and speak her mind. She never said, "Frank, you need to stay home more." Instead, she enabled his behavior.

One night, so drunk he could hardly stand, he stumbled home to their cottage. He managed to make it to the bathroom before the world spun violently around him. He emptied his evening into the toilet.

She shouted, "I hope you die."

She repeated her curses as Frank leaned over the commode. Somewhere in the depths of his drunken haze, he felt the sting of her words, but the next day, they slipped away as quickly as beer eased into his belly.

Frank graduated from UD and began working for his dad at the Dubuque Casket Company. With a modest salary, they moved into a larger house and soon welcomed two more children, Scott and Ginger, into their family.

Frank drank to excess three or four nights a week, returning home at two in the morning, his mind foggy from the night's escapades. He had no concept of how much money he squandered on beer, tips, and cigarettes. He thought he had everything under control. To him, an alcoholic was someone who woke up, popped a beer, and drank all day.

He would never admit it, but Frank was a full-blown alcoholic.

In addition to managing a busy home with three growing children, Gaye also volunteered with the Visiting Nurses Association. With a keen eye for decorating, she took a lead role managing the decor in their annual gala. There, she met plenty of women and kept busy playing tennis with them at the country club.

In the summertime, golf consumed Frank's life. He hit balls at the driving range before work. He'd return home for a quick bite to eat, then rush back to the golf course to hit balls again. After work, he'd play until darkness blanketed the sky. Every moment he was on the course, Gaye's resentment grew. Finally, hoping to find a way to spend time together, she signed up for golf lessons. She learned the fundamentals of how to swing the clubs and keep score.

Together, they signed up for couples' golf on Friday nights. Paired with another couple, they spent evenings riding from one end of the course to the other. She relished the mulligans and enjoyed "best shot" games. They looked great together.

One evening when they returned home, Gaye studied Frank's face. "What's wrong?"

"Nothing," he replied tersely.

"No, seriously. Something's going on. I learned to play golf so we could do this together, but you're out there moping around."

Frank stood with his hands on his hips. "What we're doing out there isn't golf."

"What are you talking about?"

"I'm not going to take the best ball from the group. I have no interest in blending my game with yours. I won't cheat to get a better score for the group."

Gaye's patience wore thin. "Can't you relax? It's a social thing."

He shook his head. "It's not golf."

They kept up appearances for as long as they could, but cracks formed in the facade they tried so hard to project. After that summer, they stopped playing golf together.

The chasm deepened.

Frank's drunken evenings continued until one night, after putting the kids to bed, Gaye packed his suitcase and placed it in the middle of the garage. He rolled in, and Gaye watched as he stopped his car to move the bags aside before parking. Then he calmly came inside and, without a word, slipped into bed as if the world outside didn't exist.

Another night, he came home in a drunken rage. He began to yell and raised havoc all over the house. He grabbed Gaye, and her heart raced in fear. Their daughter Gigi stirred awake and ventured into the bedroom. But her presence didn't temper Frank's fury; he continued his tirade, unchecked and wild.

Gaye managed to break free from his grasp. She gathered the kids and rushed them into the car, yelling that they were going to her brother's house. They spent the night in a motel on Highway 20, a refuge from the storm that had invaded their home.

Back at home, Frank braced himself for the unknown. Fearful of Gaye's brother's retribution, he grabbed his shotgun from the wall and loaded it with trembling hands.

Thankfully, nobody confronted him that night.

Gaye returned the next morning with their children, but the storm brewing between them raged on.

Seven years into their marriage, Frank's sister, Gretchen, noted their growing discontent. She suggested they do something for their marriage. Frank resisted, insisting everything was fine. But Gretchen persisted, practically ordering them to attend a Christian marriage encounter at a church in Saint Louis. They obeyed. With a mix of hope and trepidation, the troubled couple left their kids with Gaye's parents and set off on a Friday afternoon.

All day Saturday, Frank and Gaye sat in the conference and listened to the speaker who focused on communication skills. In small-group workshops, they wrote letters to one another and read them aloud. Emotions spilled forth as Gaye felt her feelings validated. Frank looked different. She felt a connection with her husband once again.

That night, the teacher shared the message of Jesus Christ in a way that resonated deeply with Gaye. She learned that Jesus is God, that He had died on the cross for her sins, and that through His resurrection, she could have forgiveness of her sins and eternal life. That night, she poured out her heart to Jesus Christ and asked Him to forgive her. Amazement washed over her, bringing with it a profound sense of hope and freedom, and a closeness to Frank she had not known before. As they drove home, she believed they were on the path to beautiful redemption. She began to believe their marriage could be better.

But back at home, they continued attending the same local church they had for years. The message of Jesus as Lord and Redeemer never surfaced there. The pastor never touched on the concept of a personal relationship with Christ. The teachings revolved around the faulty premise that you would enter heaven if your good deeds outweighed your bad deeds. Without mentors or guidance on how to maintain a spiritual life with Jesus at the center, Gaye and Frank returned to their old patterns.

Life fell back into its familiar rhythm. Frank resumed his drinking multiple nights a week, ignoring his wife and kids. The hope they had felt so briefly slipped through their fingers like sand.

One Sunday, a church leader approached Frank. Without any probing questions or scrutiny regarding Frank's lifestyle, he invited Frank to be an elder. Frank accepted, believing it would strengthen his connection to the church community. After Wednesday night elder meetings, Frank soon found himself at local bars, indulging in drinks and distractions. One night, he spotted another elder there.

The man's eyes widened, and he disappeared into the crowd as if trying to evade Frank. Was he ashamed of being seen there, Frank wondered. He shrugged off the idea with a laugh and grabbed another beer and a cigarette. At the next elder meeting, Frank sat across the table from the man, but neither of them mentioned the encounter.

Panic attacks had become Gaye's unwelcome but ever-present companion. The world outside felt like a prison. When she looked up at the sky, it seemed to close in around her. Her home was a sanctuary, and any place beyond its walls sent her heart racing. Buildings felt like traps. Tight spaces suffocated her. The attacks, though increasingly numerous, were unpredictable and usually lasted only twenty seconds, but each one felt like an eternity of paralyzing fear.

Frank noticed her suffering. "Gaye, let's see if a doctor can help you with your panic attacks."

The doctor ordered blood work and diagnosed her with a hyperactive thyroid and blood sugar issues. He also recommended eating six small meals a day to manage her blood sugar.

The label provided Gaye with some clarity, yet the struggles persisted. Gaye learned to recognize the creeping sensation of an impending attack and to use deep breaths to quell her anxiety, but the fear remained. So did her passive-aggressive tendencies in protesting Frank's lifestyle.

One rainy night when Frank arrived home late, he found the living room and porch lights blazing. Clothes, cascading out the front door, were strewn haphazardly across the yard. A closer look revealed that the shirts and pants cast onto the grass belonged to him. He laughed at the absurdity of the scene, ignored the disaster in the yard, pulled into the garage, and went straight to bed. The next day, Gaye collected every piece of clothing and sheepishly washed, dried, ironed, and neatly returned everything to Frank's closet and dresser.

The victimization cycle continued. Their unspoken battles persisted. Unable to speak her mind directly and without the confidence to confront him, Gaye carried on.

As their three kids matured into teenagers, Gaye found a haven in a job at a local bookstore, a relief from the chaos Frank brought home. She continued to maintain a pristine home, adorning their modest dwelling with the skill of a professional interior decorator. She made sure the kids were well fed and properly clothed, assisted with their studies, and was a constant presence at their numerous sports and theater activities.

Yet, she bore these burdens alone, working tirelessly while Frank prioritized golf and hunting. The teenagers questioned his absence, and his flimsy excuses could no longer conceal his blatant disregard for his family.

Frank took the kids with him on the golf course as caddies. He focused on his game, trying to improve his strokes. His main instruction for them was so they could provide him with the proper club for each situation. When hunting season came, he took them into the woods, and they brought home ducks, rabbits, and pheasant. But these days mirrored those that Frank had experienced with his own father, and nothing was gained.

He continued to spend his evenings away from home. Late one night at the Dodge House, the phone rang, cutting through the haze of laughter and clinking glasses. Shelly, the bartender, handed Frank the receiver. "It's for you."

He grabbed the receiver with a smile. "Hello?"

Gaye's voice cut through the noise. "You need to come home now, Frank."

"I'll be home soon." Then he ordered another round.

After that, whenever Gaye called (which became frequent), Shelly covered for him, telling her Frank wasn't there. When Frank eventually stumbled home, Gaye accused him of sleeping with Shelly. Week after week, Gaye pressed the issue, insisting he was having an affair. Frank dodged her questions and avoided confrontation, but the tension thickened.

One night, he leaned in closer to Shelly than usual, drawn into the flirtation. When closing time arrived, he let loose a stream of compliments, and she invited him to her place.

He accepted.

The next day, shame clung to him like a heavy fog. He knew what he had done was wrong and couldn't look her in the eye. He switched bars, abandoning the Dodge House and Shelly for good.

A few months later, Frank was reminiscing with old friends, and one of them mentioned a girl Frank had dated in college. "She's back in town. Do you want to meet up?"

His mind screamed, "That's weird," yet his mouth betrayed him. "Sure."

They met for drinks, and the laughter flowed as they caught up on years apart. Nothing physical transpired, but the connection lingered. Two months later, they met again. This time, the conversation flowed into the night, and as the drinks dulled their senses, she leaned closer and asked, "Would you like to go back to my place?"

"Yes." The word tumbled out before he could stop it.

It was painfully clear: Frank and Gaye's marriage was crumbling. Divorce loomed ahead like a dark cloud. Everyone saw it. Friends would have bet money on their inevitable split.

Frank quietly arranged an appointment with his attorney. He poured out his story, concluding with, "I want a divorce."

"No, you don't," the lawyer replied, raising an index finger.

"Why do you say that?" Frank asked.

"Who will the kids live with? Think about splitting your assets." He outlined the financial mess a divorce would create.

Frank felt a splitting headache.

"You'll likely remarry. Gaye will too. Now you've got blended families to deal with."

Frank hung his head.

"Where will the kids go at Christmas? How will they celebrate their birthdays?"

"You're right. That's not what I want." Frank slumped back in his chair, arms hanging limply at his sides. "What do I do?"

"Frank, I make a living doing this. If you want a divorce, I'll go through it with you. But you shouldn't do it."

Frank left the office discouraged and confused. Somehow, a flicker of determination ignited within him. He decided to fight for his marriage.

Gaye was also at the end of herself. Convinced it was time to take charge of her life, she made an appointment with a lawyer. Their conversation mirrored what Frank had gone through, with the same conclusion. Gaye left the polished, mahogany-lined office disoriented. What now?

They were both stuck.

Hopeless.

Would they have to endure this turmoil for the rest of their lives?

Despite their train wreck of a marriage, Frank worked tirelessly at the Dubuque Casket Company, pouring his efforts into growing the company. During his trips to Des Moines, he found himself a familiar guest at the Executive Hotel, where a woman caught his attention. They hit it off at an office dinner, and an easy camaraderie began. Later, they gathered for drinks at their host's house. There, Frank lounged on the couch with her while their host disappeared into the bedroom with a woman who wasn't his wife.

As they talked, the woman set a boundary for Frank. "I never date married men." The predator in him heard those words as a challenge.

A month later at their next business meeting, he stayed with her three nights in a row.

Driving home, Frank passed endless cornfields and tractors plowing soil that looked as desolate as his conscience. Deep down, he knew what he was doing with this woman in Des Moines was wrong. Guilt piled high and overwhelmed him.

Why had he crossed that line?

The lady in Des Moines was a victim, just like Gaye.

He loved Gaye. He adored their three incredible kids.

He wrestled with his thoughts. Should he break it off? The time he'd spent with this new lady was intoxicating. Ending it would hurt her, and he didn't want that.

Maybe he could keep going this way. After all, Gaye didn't know. He wasn't hurting anyone. In a moment of desperation he called out, "God, is it possible to love two women at the same time?"

The response reverberated in his heart, a resounding *NO*.

It wasn't an audible voice. He didn't see clouds in the sky forming letters. Yet, in his spirit, he felt a colossal no.

No. No ifs, ands, or buts—just *no*.

Frank faced a pivotal moment. It was time to confront his reality.

A few weeks later, Gaye marched down the stairs, her footsteps resolute. Frank sprawled in front of the television, eyes glued to a golf tournament. She didn't waste a second. "Frank, this marriage stinks.

I'm going to see a counselor. If you want to come with me, that's fine. If not, I don't care. I need to find out what's going on."

Frank glanced at her, his mind already forming an idea of what counseling might accomplish. *It might be a good thing*, he thought. *If I can get her fixed, then all this nonsense will be behind us.*

But Gaye's arms, folded tightly across her chest, indicated she wasn't interested in halfhearted attention. She waited, unwavering.

Finally, he shrugged. "All right. I'll go with you."

Gaye found a marriage counselor named Bob Rowe in the phone book and scheduled their first session. They entered his office, both uncertain and tense. Within thirty minutes, Frank's initial notion of "fixing" Gaye began to unravel. Bob's words shifted his perspective, and his questions peeled back layers Frank hadn't considered in years. He began to see himself as at least half of the problem.

They met with Bob once a month, learning the tools of open communication, active listening, and ways to express needs and feelings. As a secular counselor, Bob gave them standard, reliable methods to start chipping away at the distance between them. It brought some relief, but even with this newfound understanding, Frank's life held a secret undercurrent. He was still traveling frequently to Des Moines and slipping away into his adulterous world each time.

Frank and Gaye met with Bob six times, paying a hefty bill. Seeing no real progress, however, they canceled their next appointment and did not reschedule.

About a year later, things reached a boiling point. Frank stumbled home, the smell of alcohol following him in, and Gaye's patience finally gave way. They argued, words slashing, anger pouring out of both of them until Gaye couldn't stand it any longer. Angry, hurt, and overwhelmed, she grabbed the car keys, stormed out to the garage, and flung herself into the driver's seat. She slammed her foot on the accelerator and backed out into the icy night, needing to get as far away as possible. But in her rush, the Toyota slid on the snowy driveway and wedged itself into a storm drain. She tried putting it in drive, pressing the gas hard. The tires spun, uselessly whirring in place. She shifted to reverse, the same result.

Frustration washed over her as she tried again, her rage and sorrow spilling out in sobs. She looked up to see Frank walking toward her, his expression unreadable. He stopped by the driver's side window, glanced at her red-rimmed eyes, and surveyed the car. Then he shook his head, turned, and headed back into the house, leaving her alone in the cold.

Gaye gripped the steering wheel as tears spilled down her face, the weight of their years heavy on her shoulders. She dropped her head back against the headrest and declared, "That's it. I'm done. Just done." In that moment, something hardened within her.

She wouldn't care about Frank anymore, she decided. He'd spent years coming and going as he pleased, staying out with his buddies until all hours. Now, it was her turn.

The next weekend, Gaye put on her nicest slacks and a sweater that fit just right. She studied herself in the mirror. She looked good, and she knew it. For once, Frank stayed home with the kids, and she stepped out with her girlfriends, feeling a rebellious thrill. She wanted to see if men noticed her and if they would look twice. Part of her hoped it would get under Frank's skin and force him to notice her again, but nothing changed. Frank continued his familiar habits, and Gaye began forming her own.

She and her friends hit various bars, dancing into the night. She'd sit at the bar, catch a stranger's eye, and watch as a drink was sent her way. Each drink was a thrilling reminder that she could still be seen, still admired. But when any man tried to approach, a spike of fear would pierce her and she'd make an excuse to leave. She didn't want a relationship, didn't even want to talk. She wasn't ready to let anyone in. She just needed to know she could … if she wanted to.

Truth be told, Gaye rarely felt at ease around anyone. Well, except one person—a longtime friend, handsome, and comfortable in a way that others weren't. He brought none of the anxieties of starting over with someone new and reminded her of Frank in just enough ways to make things easy. Gaye also knew his wife; they were casual friends.

That's all it was—they were just friends.

Until one day, descending the steps of a local bar, she spotted him on the landing. His eyes lit up as he saw her.

"Wow, you're looking good today."

His words lingered in her mind, filling an empty space she hadn't known was there. The feeling struck with a simple but powerful validation.

They continued to cross paths, each encounter drawing them closer. He was easy to talk to, quick with a kind word, expected nothing in return—he offered exactly what she needed. But as they continued to talk and interact, the connection between them grew stronger.

Finally, with quiet resolve, she found a way to meet him in private.

When she arrived at his house, anticipation filled the air. They had their first physical encounter, an experience that both awakened and comforted her in unexpected ways. This continued for months.

CHAPTER SEVEN

Ugly Truths

Between Frank and Gaye, things continued to grow worse, until the day when Gaye confronted Frank about his affair, and they had the biggest and worst fight of their lives. Their ugly truths spilled into the open. Frank's affair was laid bare, and in the heat of their fight, Gaye confessed her own affair. Their marriage, worn and battered, now stood stripped to its fragile core. Exhausted, they knelt together on the bench at the end of their bed, no defenses left.

"God"—Frank's voice broke in prayer—"God, we don't know how to do this. We want to stay together, but we have no clue how to go forward." For a long time, silence filled the room, heavy and uncertain. Neither knew what step to take next.

Finally, Frank spoke up. "I'll call Gretchen." He dialed her number, and after recounting the story, he listened, nodded, and then hung up. "She'll be here tomorrow."

The next afternoon, Gretchen and her husband, Mike, arrived from South Dakota. They exchanged pleasantries and caught up on the kids and life ... and avoided the deep conversation everyone knew was coming. That evening, they all sat down together at Perkins. They were still perusing the menu when Gretchen's gaze grew intense.

"You guys have both asked Christ into your life," she said, "but you've never made Him Lord of your life."

Frank let out a weary sigh. "What does that mean?"

Gretchen leaned in. "Being a Christ follower isn't about saying the sinner's prayer and assuming it's all good. It's about choosing to live life His way, not yours."

Frank stared at his sister. "What are you talking about?"

She held his gaze. "Frank, tell me, what does it mean to be a Christian?"

He shifted uncomfortably and repeated the message he'd first heard from Billy Graham on TV many years earlier. "God sent Jesus, His only Son, to take our place when He died on the cross. He was placed in the tomb, arose three days later, and defeated death. He forgives our sins, and we have everlasting life with Him."

"Right." Gretchen's eyes didn't soften. "But it doesn't stop there. You have to make Jesus the Lord of your life. That means you actually have to follow Him. It's more than just words. It's changing how you live, replacing your desires with His teachings ..."

She looked pointedly at Frank, then at Gaye. "Right now, you're ignoring His commands and living on your own terms."

Frank exchanged a glance with Gaye.

Gretchen leaned back. "How's that working out for you?"

Frank lowered his head, defeated. Gaye focused intently on her napkin. The waiter returned, oblivious to the gravity of the conversation. They gave their orders and he left. Silence settled around the table.

After a minute, Gretchen continued, her tone firm. "God loves you both, but He wants every part of you. When you follow His ways, that's when things start to work."

Frank leaned forward and asked some questions. Gretchen responded with specific directives. By the time the meal ended, Frank and Gaye could see the beginning of a fuller picture, a path forward illuminated by faith.

Gretchen led them in a simple prayer, her words steady and clear. "God, You are now Lord of our lives. We won't rely on our own decisions anymore. We look to You for everything."

Frank looked up. "So, if I'm going to make Jesus Lord of my life, how do I start?"

Gretchen didn't hesitate. "You need to end things with that woman tonight."

Frank gave a slow nod. He'd assured Gaye it was over, but she wasn't surprised he hadn't truly cut ties yet.

Setting down her fork, Gretchen ordered, "Let's go to your office and call her."

With no words left, Frank paid the bill. Frank and Gaye obediently followed, driving in silence to his office, where Gretchen and Mike waited in the small lobby as Frank picked up the phone.

Frank shuffled through papers unnecessarily; he knew her number. He shifted from foot to foot, but finally dialed and raised the receiver. Gaye picked up the secretary's line to listen in.

"Hi. This is Frank."

"Hi, Frank! It's good to hear your voice."

He cleared his throat. "I'm here with my wife, Gaye, on the other line. I want you to know this is real."

Silence.

Frank continued. "I don't know how else to say this, but it's over. Gaye and I have agreed to work on our marriage. We're bringing it together, and you can't be a part of it. This ends here." He hung up.

Relief washed over Gaye like a refreshing rain after years of drought. It was over.

Frank turned to her. "I know you don't trust me right now, but I'll do whatever it takes to rebuild that. I still have a business center in Des Moines. I'll have to go there."

Gaye stood motionless, absorbing his words, not sure how to respond.

Frank steadied himself. "I'm not going tomorrow, but the business trips will have to happen eventually. If you want me to stop on the way and call you every five minutes, I'll do it."

Gaye let out a small, incredulous laugh. She knew that was impractical, even absurd. Pulling over to call every few miles seemed pointless.

He pressed on. "If you'd rather come with me, that's fine. Or send one of the kids. Whatever makes you feel safe."

Gaye nodded slowly. "We'll figure something out."

With Gretchen's watchful gaze upon him, he added, "I mean it, Gaye. Whatever it takes."

The morning after their dinner at Perkins, Gaye prepared a simple breakfast for Gretchen and Mike. As they sat at the table, an odd calm settled over them.

Gretchen looked at Gaye. "Gaye, you know the woman, the wife of the man you had an affair with?"

Gaye's heart pounded. Shame tightened her throat, and she nodded.

"You need to go to her house, confess what happened, and ask for forgiveness."

"Are you sure?" Gaye's mouth went dry. "Do I really have to do that?"

Gretchen didn't waver. "You do."

Fear welled up within her. She couldn't speak. She knew this conversation would be devastating. She knew herself the pain she was about to inflict, and no words or apologies could soften the blow. Her thoughts spiraled, and shame swallowed her whole.

That evening, Gaye and Frank drove to the couple's home. They walked up to the door, feeling the weight of what lay ahead, and knocked. When the door opened, the couple greeted them with a warmth that felt out of place. "Hey, you two, come on in."

Gaye's voice trembled. "I'm sorry, we're not here with pleasant news."

The wife looked puzzled, the husband uneasy.

They all sat down, and Gaye turned to her friend, willing herself to get the words out. "Please forgive me for the adultery I committed with your husband."

The woman's eyes went wide, flicking to her husband in utter shock.

He looked away. "It's been over for a long time," he muttered.

The woman's expression crumpled, her pain surfacing in anguished sobs. Tears streamed down Gaye's face, too, as she was consumed by shame and guilt. No words could bridge the divide between them.

The woman's sobs turned to raw, visceral cries. Frank, unable to bear the weight of her suffering, felt compelled to speak as if confessing could somehow validate her pain. "I had an affair, too."

"So? What am I supposed to do?" The woman's grief flared into fury. "Go have sex with the whole world?"

No one dared to speak, as if the air itself had fractured under the weight of betrayal. Frank and Gaye stumbled out the door. On the drive home, neither spoke. Once back, they debriefed with Gretchen, then retreated to bed, drained and shattered.

The following day, every step felt like moving through a swamp. If not for the obligation of hosting her sister-in-law, Gaye might not have gotten up at all. Somehow, in her numb state, she made breakfast and set it on the table.

Gretchen poured syrup on her pancakes. "You two have done well."

Gaye took a sip of coffee, willing the conversation to end. She couldn't handle another task. Yet, as Gretchen took a bite, her expression turned serious. "You've taken the first few steps in what will be a long, difficult journey."

Gaye's heart sank. She knew another assignment was coming.

Sure enough, Gretchen set her fork down and stared at Frank and Gaye. "Now you need to tell your children before they hear about this from someone else."

"Are you sure?" Gaye had grown weary of Gretchen's orders.

Gretchen nodded. "This is a small community. Rumors travel. It's only a matter of time before someone says something."

Frank glanced at Gaye. "Gigi will be home from college for Easter next weekend. We'll do it then."

"You two also need to see a counselor," Gretchen added.

Gaye shrugged. "We did that. Six times, and it wasn't free. We were throwing our money away."

"How long have you two been drifting apart?"

Frank shrugged. "Years."

Gretchen cradled her coffee mug. "Look, you've made a good start, but there isn't a quick fix. It could take years of hard work to straighten everything out. You have many issues to get to the bottom of and understand. Find a Christian counselor. If the first one you see isn't having you do the work, find another. If you commit to seek the Lord in your marriage, learn what you need to learn, and do the hard work, you two can fall in love all over again."

Gretchen and Mike left not long after, and Frank and Gaye scheduled an appointment with their pastor. Then they mapped out how they would tell their children and seek forgiveness, however long that might take. When Easter arrived and Gigi came home, they savored a few hours of normalcy, grasping at the fleeting comfort. But soon, they gathered the kids in the living room. Frank began.

"It's essential that you hear this from us. Your mom and I … we've both committed adultery."

And they recounted the events, leaving no detail unaddressed—Gaye's confrontation with Frank, their individual infidelities, the lessons Gretchen had impressed upon them, Frank's phone call to end his affair, and Gaye's confession to her friend. Every revelation weighed heavily in the air. The children listened, faces flushed, jaws set. Tears filled their eyes as the truth settled in.

Frank looked from one child to the next. "We've come to the end of ourselves. We're going to work on this marriage, no matter what. Divorce is not an option."

Gaye's voice broke as she looked at her children. "We beg you to forgive us for everything we've put you through."

No one said anything, and shame wrapped around Gaye like a blanket. Parents weren't supposed to bring this kind of heartbreak into their children's lives.

Frank broke the silence. "You don't have to forgive us now. If you have questions, ask us anytime. We'll answer honestly."

The kids drifted to their rooms without a word, leaving the couple alone with the wreckage they'd exposed.

Weeks passed. When Gigi came home from college on another break, she sought out her mom. With a tear-streaked face she said, "We know you two have always fought, but I forgive you, and I'm proud you're staying together to work this out."

In time, Scott and Ginger came forward, echoing Gigi's words. They only asked to keep the other people's names from them. They didn't want the knowledge or the images it would bring. Not long after, one of Gigi's friends approached her, revealing the rumors she'd heard. Gigi held her head high as she responded, "My parents are already working on their marriage."

Years later, Gaye and Frank learned that as they'd sat their children down that Easter Sunday, the kids had braced for the worst. Divorce had seemed inevitable. But instead, they'd been given a small glimmer of hope, a sliver of certainty amid the chaos.

For the next several months, Frank and Gaye leaned into their commitment. Gaye joined Frank on several of his business trips, and Scott went along twice. If he was alone, Frank called from wherever he was staying, giving updates, staying connected, and rebuilding the bridge one conversation at a time.

Under Gretchen's relentless instruction, Frank and Gaye reached out for professional support too. Their initial visits with the counselors revealed how much more complex the process would be than they'd imagined.

CHAPTER EIGHT

Counselors and Conferences

Pastor Ivan listened intently, his expression shifting as Frank and Gaye's story unfolded before him. His eyes widened, and he crossed his arms, clearly realizing this wasn't a problem with a simple solution. After a moment of silence, he offered a suggestion—"My wife would be a good person for you two to talk to."

A week later, they found themselves back in his office, this time with his wife. Her reaction was calm, not as surprised and alarmed as her husband's had been. She assured them she had worked with couples in similar situations before. With a steady voice, she outlined a series of exercises using a blend of communication tools. Some resembled prior suggestions they'd heard, others appeared to be more coping method than anything else.

It all felt nebulous, like grasping at the mist, yet they clung to the hope that with enough effort, things might improve. After every meeting, Gretchen called for an update, insisting on talking with both Frank and Gaye. Frank told her what they'd talked about, and Gretchen piled on further instructions.

They visited Pastor Ivan's wife for six weeks, faithfully completing her assignments, yet no identifiable change came.

In frustration, Frank called another local pastor and made an appointment. Within a few days, Frank and Gaye sat across from Pastor Bill and recounted their story. Bill's face revealed little as the details poured out. When they finally finished, he stood up and crossed to the other side of his desk, positioning himself directly in front of Frank. He said, "You're walking with a foot in both camps. The Lord will not honor that. You need to make a decision."

The gravity in Bill's words cut through to Frank's core.

Frank replied, "I'll do whatever it takes."

"Start by reading the Bible and praying." He gave them a Bible reading plan and simple instructions to find a solitary place to reach out to God in prayer for an extended period of time each day.

Frank grappled with this new directive. The scriptures felt foreign, and prayer seemed like an exercise in futility. His mind spun, searching for structure, a clear set of rules, and a path to success. He tried it, reading here and there, offering up a few prayers. But it all felt hollow and mechanical. They started attending Bill's church, absorbing his teachings week after week, but the progress felt slow.

At their next meeting, when Bill inquired about their efforts, Frank hesitated, then exaggerated his progress, giving Bill the impression of greater dedication. Bill, sensing their need for additional guidance, suggested they attend a marriage conference. Frank nodded along, though the concept was foreign to him. Conferences were for business, learning about products, or networking over rounds of golf. A conference to talk about relationships and marriage was uncharted territory.

They found a weekend event in Wheaton, Illinois, led by Leanne Payne, a prominent author on healing, forgiveness, and listening prayer.

Arriving at the conference, Frank felt a mixture of obligation and curiosity. He held on to a cautious hope for some breakthrough, while Gaye, in contrast, was open to anything and prepared to embrace whatever might unfold.

They slipped in quietly and took seats near the back. The session began with worship. Song after song filled the space. Frank expected teaching to follow soon, but the music continued, flowing like a river that didn't end. Around them, people began speaking in tongues. Others interpreted, translating strange, unfamiliar words as the congregation swayed in unity. It stretched on, a relentless wave of prayer and worship.

Finally, Leanne Payne took the stage, her presence commanding yet gentle. She spoke about a concept Frank had never considered: listening. Not just listening to your spouse, but listening to God. Leanne led them in a session of listening prayer, guiding them to quiet their hearts and listen for God's voice. They left with practical tools, a new approach to seeking God and recognizing His voice in the stillness. This experience was like nothing they had encountered before, a unique spiritual territory, rich and unfamiliar.

At home, Gaye created a prayer nook by the back window, filling the space with books and her Bible. She began recording her prayers in her journal, returning daily to connect with Jesus. Frank pressed in as well, but instead of spending an extended period of time in prayer alone, he forged his own style. He began talking to God throughout the day, like he would if he were visiting with a close friend.

Frank and Gaye returned to hear Leanne speak at another conference. She instructed them to bow their heads and pray, inviting them to ask God to reveal who He was. Gaye prayed, unsure what to expect. "What do You have for me?"

Then came a sensation that she might receive a prayer language. She recoiled. "No, no, no, I don't want that weird stuff."

But an inner calm overrode her resistance. Slowly, she surrendered, letting the tension drain from her mind and body. In that release, words formed, unfamiliar sounds spilled out, their meaning a mystery. Yet she somehow knew that she was speaking to God directly, not in her own language but in a language beyond her understanding.

Back home, in addition to a new life revolving around prayer, Frank and Gaye dove into books on marriage and relationships. *Healing the Shame that Binds You,* by John Bradshaw, taught that shame itself often fuels toxic behaviors, compulsions, codependencies, and addictions that can chip away at lives and marriages. They soon found themselves attending one of Bradshaw's conferences, overwhelmed, yet hungry for more.

Their appetite for learning grew. They picked up more books and sought wisdom from reputable teachers. Eventually, they signed up for a conference led by Dan Allender, a respected voice on relationships, blending psychology and Christian principles. This session focused entirely on shame, and they filled their suitcase with every book on the topic they could find.

In addition to the conferences on marriage, Gretchen recommended they attend a conference focused on healing. Far from their comfort zone, they settled into seats at the back, watching the small crowd of a hundred or so people. Delores Winder, a petite woman with dark hair and quiet strength, took the stage and shared her own miraculous story:

once immobilized in a full-body cast, she had been completely healed. Her husband then guided everyone through a scriptural teaching on healing. After worship, Delores began calling out attendees, describing their ailments without prior knowledge, and inviting them to come forward for healing. As she prayed, Frank and Gaye saw people healed from sicknesses. They exchanged glances, astonished.

That evening, while staying down the hall from Delores and Bill, they were pleasantly surprised when Delores invited them over for ice cream. The small gathering felt casual, even comforting.

"How are you two feeling?" Delores asked.

Frank shrugged. "This is all new to us."

Delores and Bill patiently answered their questions, gently guiding them through the basics of healing ministry.

After a pause, Delores turned to Frank. "I'd like to pray for you."

Frank shifted uncomfortably. "For what?"

"Smoking," she said.

Frank grimaced. "I've tried to quit dozens of times. But every time I try, I get so grumpy everyone around me suffers."

Delores asked, "How much do you smoke?"

Gaye answered, "Three packs a day."

Delores nodded. "How much does it affect your health?"

"Not at all," Frank insisted.

Gaye interjected. "You cough all the time, Frank." She turned to Delores, her voice wavering. "Every time I hear him cough, I think he's going to die."

Delores glanced between them. "Frank, may I pray for you?"

He conceded. "I guess so."

Delores placed her hands gently on his shoulders, beginning a quiet prayer. Frank listened halfheartedly, only vaguely aware of her words, waiting for it to end.

The next day, he felt the craving for cigarettes even more intensely. He spent the day ducking behind buildings, chain-smoking. Shame settled over him for failing to find the faith to overcome his addiction. That night, Delores invited them back for ice cream.

"How's it going, Frank?" she asked kindly.

Frank sighed. "I thought I'd quit after you prayed. It didn't work. Today, I smoked even more than usual. I couldn't resist."

Delores smiled. "Frank, didn't you hear what I prayed?"

He blinked, caught off guard. "Apparently not."

"I asked that with each cigarette you smoke, God would prepare you for the day He tells you to quit and heals you back to the health you had when you started."

Frank paused, the weight of her words sinking in. "You mean, restore me to how I was at thirteen, smoking Lucky Strikes with the other caddies?"

Delores nodded with a smile. "Exactly. When you quit, your body will be like you never smoked at all."

The pressure lifted. He laughed, realizing the grace in her words.

Then Delores turned to Gaye. "I'd like to pray for you, too."

Gaye hesitated. "I'm fine, really."

Delores looked at her gently. "I want to pray about your fear of Frank dying from smoking."

Tears spilled down Gaye's cheeks. Frank watched with surprise. He hadn't realized the weight of her fear. Delores placed her hands on Gaye's head, praying for her release from that heavy burden. When she finished, Gaye breathed deeply, freed from a specific worry that had plagued her for years.

They went home, and Frank continued smoking pack after pack on the golf course without another thought of quitting. A few months later, however, early one Tuesday morning, he realized he was down to his last cigarette and drove to the closest store. He pushed open the door, stepping over the store's worn wooden floorboards.

"Can I get a carton of Marlboros, please?"

The cashier shrugged apologetically. "We're almost out. Should have more on Thursday."

Frank bought their remaining packs, enough to last a day. On Thursday morning, with only two cigarettes left, he returned. "Any Marlboros today?"

The cashier shook her head. "Driver came by, but he didn't leave any."

Disappointed, Frank turned to leave. As he pushed open the door, he felt a jolt—a sudden force as if someone had struck the back of his head. He spun around, looking for the source, but saw only the empty store. In that instant, he knew. God was telling him it was time to quit.

The craving vanished.

No withdrawal, no struggle.

He tossed his last two cigarettes in the trash, drove home, and walked in the door. "I just quit smoking," he announced, and his voice held a certainty he hadn't felt before.

Gaye's eyes widened. "What?"

"God told me to quit," he explained. "I threw the rest of my cigarettes away."

It was a miracle, plain as day.

Months later, he passed a Marlboro billboard on the freeway. A fierce, almost primal urge to smoke assailed him. He could taste the cigarette and feel the familiar burn in his throat. Confused, he realized he was under a spiritual attack. An unseen force tempted him.

Frank prayed. "I bind you, Satan, in Jesus's name. Lord, keep those cigarettes away from me."

Peace washed over him. The desire faded as suddenly as it had come. From then on, he was free of tobacco and remained amazingly healthy.

In addition to his other social circles, Frank was also a proud member of the "I-Club." The Dubuque Golf and Country Club regularly hosted this gathering, bringing in speakers from the University of Iowa's football team. Coaches and trainers would share game insights, show films, and walk members through the highs and lows of the season. It was a dream for any Hawkeye fan and a thrill for Frank.

One day, the routine of film analysis and game updates was set aside. The speaker took the stage and began sharing his own story. He spoke of high school years spent in sobriety, only to take up drinking in college. "I always drank beer because I knew nobody could load my drinks. I was in control of not being in control. Weekends of college drinking turned into weekend drinking as an adult, and then, over time, drinking became a fixture during my week. Tuesday nights after golf, Wednesday nights with the guys, and Thursday nights. Each time, I drank more. I could never stop at just a few beers."

Frank recognized himself in the man's words. With each admission, it became more apparent that this man's story mirrored Frank's story.

The speaker went on to talk about how alcohol had strained his marriage, distanced him from his children, and ultimately dismantled his life. At the end, he said it plainly: "I'm an alcoholic."

The words hit Frank hard.

The thought of it followed him from the golf club, leaving him too unsettled to return to work. Instead, he drove home, the question echoing in his mind: What does this mean about me?

When he got home, he told Gaye, "I think I'm an alcoholic."

"No, you're not," she said.

But Frank couldn't ignore it. The Lord was pressing him to acknowledge the truth. "I think I am, Gaye. I'm going to quit drinking for six months."

She was surprised but supportive. He asked her for help, explaining how difficult it would be when they went to their friends' houses, where the expectation to drink was ingrained. "They're going to come down on me hard," he told her. "I don't know that I can do it alone."

Gaye agreed to back him up.

That Friday night, the test began. Frank walked into the kitchen and grabbed a can of Pepsi from the fridge. It took only seconds for his friends to notice. "Frank, what's wrong with you?" one asked.

"Put that down," another friend demanded. "Grab a Coors."

Frank kept calm. "Relax. I quit drinking," he replied. They laughed, began teasing him, accused him of being henpecked.

Gaye overheard the jabs, and her patience ran thin. She stepped in, pointing her finger at each of them. "Frank's trying to quit. He's a good man trying to do life right, and you guys are just piling on."

They backed down, and Frank felt Gaye's strength in that moment. He sipped his Pepsi and held his ground.

As the weeks passed, Frank began to see his friends differently. Each weekend, he watched as they laughed too loudly, told the same stories, and replayed their old glories as if each tale was a revelation.

By the end of the evening, they seemed foolish and redundant, locked in a cycle they couldn't see.

He asked Gaye, "Did I act like that when I was drinking?"

"You were worse," she said.

Frank held to his vow for six months, turning down drinks and avoiding the old routines. He slipped up twice, spending a couple of nights out drinking with his friends, but overall, he kept his resolve. At the end of his trial period, he thought he'd found a strategy: he'd limit himself to just two beers.

"It's the third beer that keeps me going all night," he told Gaye.

She nodded, hopeful it could work.

They tested his new idea on their next outing. But two beers became three, then more, until Frank was back where he'd started. Another week, another attempt, and Frank found himself drunk yet again. Driving home afterward, he lost control on Kaufman Avenue, spun out, and wrecked their new car.

The following day he realized he'd risked his life and the lives of others just for the empty thrill of drinking. The crash sobered him more than the physical impact.

"I can't go on like this," he admitted to himself. He stopped to pray and spent time listening.

Finally, he heard God's voice in his heart, "Frank, did you ever think that a lot of the issues you have are caused by your drinking?"

The realization came with a weighty certainty. He couldn't just drink less or limit his outings. He had to stop entirely.

From that day forward, Frank has never had another beer.

He didn't attend meetings. Never followed a twelve-step program. He didn't label himself as a recovering alcoholic or even as an alcoholic anymore. Instead, he accepted that he'd once had alcoholism, and God had taken it away.

For Frank, quitting was a journey he'd taken with purpose. Alcohol was gone from his life. Despite that progress, however, Frank and Gaye continued to struggle in their relationship. Decades of destructive patterns remained intact. Their problems were much deeper than they knew.

One day, after a long hard day at a golf tournament, Frank climbed in the car and sat behind the wheel. He wiped his brow as he started the engine. "Let's stop for a burger."

Gaye said, "There's a new place not far from here, I saw on the way. Have you heard of Taco Bell?"

"No," he replied. "Sounds like Mexican. I don't want Mexican food. Do you think they have burgers?"

"It's fast food," she reasoned. "All fast-food places have burgers, don't they?"

So they parked and walked inside, where they were greeted by a menu filled with Mexican dishes. Not a single hamburger in sight.

Frank turned on Gaye. "You lied to me."

"What?" She flinched, startled. "No. I didn't know."

His face burned in anger. He headed back to the car without ordering. She followed apologetically.

Frank slammed his fist on the dashboard. "I can't believe you lied to me!" He pounded the dashboard again and again. Not another word was spoken on the hour-long drive home. In fact, the seething silence stretched on for three days.

Gaye continued to walk on eggshells. Though she knew they were making progress, it was two steps forward, one step back.

CHAPTER NINE

Guilt and Shame

As Frank and Gaye put in the work, they finally began seeing progress. Gretchen continued to call regularly, and one day she encouraged them to attend a conference with a teacher she knew well, Jeff VanVonderen. She was eager for them to experience his teachings firsthand. The only problem was that the conference was far enough away that they would have to fly. Gaye felt torn. She wanted to go but couldn't imagine flying. Panic attacks were still a regular part of her life, and the idea of facing one triggered by the enclosed space of a plane was overwhelming. Even closing a bathroom door could be too much at times.

They called Gretchen the night before the flight, and Gaye admitted her fear. "It's more than simple claustrophobia. I don't know if I can get on that plane."

Gretchen said, "Let's pray." Together, they asked for God's peace, for angels to surround the plane, and for Gaye to feel safe.

The following day, Gaye was still scared, yet resolute. Tissues in hand, she clung to Frank's arm as they walked the ramp to the plane.

Each step demanded every ounce of courage she had. She stopped before boarding and whispered another silent prayer.

Her heart pounded. *I can't do this,* her mind protested. But somehow, she stepped onto the plane. She took her seat and buckled in, but her mind churned between fear and determination.

If I really have to get out of here, they'll land the plane for me.

Her anxiety surged again as the plane taxied down the runway. She looked out the window and froze. There were angels, hovering around the wing. She could see them. They glowed in radiant, iridescent hues, exuding warmth and calm. She couldn't look away. God had put them there; He'd peeled back the spiritual realm so she could see them.

Her breathing slowed. Her heart steadied.

God had sent these messengers of peace to carry her safely through this moment. She relaxed back into her seat, feeling a profound sense of safety and love. She flew in peace to the conference and back.

Jeff VanVonderen taught all day about grace, acceptance, and the power of vulnerability as antidotes to shame, ways to unlock freedom, and begin the process of restoration. In the evening, Jeff joined Gretchen, Frank, and Gaye for dinner. Around the table, Gaye and Frank shared their questions, struggles, and pieces of their journey. Then Jeff poured out his wisdom.

The concept of shame, especially as Jeff described it, stirred something deep within Gaye. As he spoke, memories began to surface from a place she had long ago shut off—painful memories, ones she had hidden even from herself. She hadn't fully understood them as a child, but looking back now, she realized how much she'd carried from those experiences.

One feeling was more potent than anything else: shame.

When her neighbor had exposed himself to her, demanding things no child should endure, shame had slithered in. It told her she was somehow at fault, inherently wrong, and unworthy. Guilt hadn't entered her mind. She hadn't done anything to feel guilty for. But shame painted a darker, more sinister picture. Over time, she had come to believe she was damaged, dirty, isolated, and powerless. Her very core had absorbed the lie that she was worthless, deserving of neglect and mistreatment. Those beliefs had colored her life for fifty-five long years.

As Jeff spoke, he illuminated a difference that struck her hard—the difference between shame and guilt. Guilt was about behavior, a signal from God that could lead to growth and change. Guilt whispered, "You've made a mistake." It pointed out specific actions to make right, offering a pathway to forgiveness and healing. Shame, however, took aim at the soul itself, eroding a person's sense of worth and identity. It wasn't about an act but about an identity. It boldly declared, "*You* are the mistake."

Jeff explained that shame came not from God but from darkness. It was a lie that sought to isolate, diminish, and destroy. While guilt had the power to bring a person closer to God through repentance, shame drove them deeper into self-doubt, sometimes into destructive behaviors or endless cycles of self-criticism.

A strange kind of relief filled Gaye as the wall she'd built around her wounds cracked open. After years of silence, she felt seen, as though someone were speaking directly to her hidden pain. Fifty-five years of shame wouldn't dissolve overnight. Gaye knew that. But finally, she had a path forward.

"Two separate thoughts can go through your mind," Jeff said. "One is *I did something bad*. This is guilt, and it's from God. God gives us guilt for wrongdoings that we need to repent of. That leads us to the foot of the cross for God's forgiveness.

"The other thought is *I am bad*. That is shame, and it's straight from Satan. Shame is feeling inherently bad about yourself as a person. It's a toxic belief that undermines self-worth. Shame leads to destructive patterns of coping, such as addiction, perfectionism, or self-sabotage. Addressing shame is incredibly important in the process of recovery from addiction or trauma. Healing from shame involves recognizing its presence, challenging negative self-beliefs, and cultivating self-compassion and acceptance. It also involves building healthy relationships and finding support from others who can provide empathy and understanding. Addressing shame is an integral part of the journey toward fostering greater self-awareness, resilience, and emotional well-being.

"Guilt is a gift from God. Something you can address, and it points to behavior to fix. Shame is from the pit of hell." Jeff stopped and looked at his listeners. "So how do you get rid of it? You pull it out of the dark and into the light."

They continued discussing the steps on a journey to freedom, one at a time, starting with bringing shame out of hiding. Shame can't live in the light. When you figure out where it came from and bring it into the light, then God can deal with it.

Gaye had a lot to think about. Healing would mean challenging every lie she'd internalized. It would mean allowing herself to lean on God's grace. It would mean embracing the truth of her inherent worth—something she'd never thought of before.

Neither Frank nor Gaye fully understood it yet, but the process had already begun. Of course, with decades of shame, it wasn't wholly reversed in a single weekend. Over the next several years, Frank and Gaye poured over books on marriage and shame, traveling to conferences and consuming material until they could nearly deliver the lectures themselves. Each new author and each speaker brought fresh nuance, often revisiting familiar themes but always sparking a new insight.

At another VanVonderen conference, they sought an appointment with him directly. His calendar was packed, but his office suggested Mary, one of his trusted associates. If Jeff endorsed her, they figured she must be skilled.

Mary listened with genuine empathy as they recounted their story. They got to know Mary well over the course of several visits. She guided them through familiar concepts, adding stories from her own life to illustrate the ideas, but she didn't do anything to address their shame. On their eighth visit, Mary opened up and revealed her personal struggles. She seemed particularly supportive of her female clients, often affirming them while taking a harder line with the husbands.

That night, Gretchen called while they were eating dinner. Frank explained what had happened, then said, "I think Mary is struggling with abandonment. Her own wounds from childhood aren't resolved."

"It feels like her counseling is tied up with her personal need for validation," Gaye added. "It's almost as if helping others helps her make sense of her own hurt. Really, it makes me wonder. Can counselors only take us as far as they've gone themselves?"

"Well," Gretchen said, "counselors are just people trying to help other people."

"Hmmm." Gaye pressed her lips together. "I think we're done with Mary."

Frank nodded. "What now?"

"Maybe God has someone else for us." Gaye said.

A few weeks passed. Then, one evening when Frank got off the phone with Gretchen, he turned to Gaye with an odd expression.

Gaye asked, "What's going on?"

"Gretchen and Mike are in counseling. They've been going through their own rough patch."

She raised an eyebrow. "Gretchen, making her husband crazy? No surprise there."

"I know she drives you nuts." Frank tilted his head to the side. "But she's my sister."

"I know."

"Okay." Frank shrugged apologetically. "Well, there is good news. They went to see a guy in Minneapolis. Gretchen says he's transformed their marriage. She thinks he could help us too."

"What's his name?"

"Paul Singh."

CHAPTER TEN

Healing in Paul's Office

Gaye called for an appointment with Paul Singh. The earliest he had was three months out, but she took it anyway. Days later, the office called back with an unexpected cancellation.

Frank and Gaye packed up and drove north to the southern suburbs of Minneapolis, pulling into a parking lot with a towering fountain spraying fifteen feet into the air. Inside, they sat in a small waiting room. When the door opened, a short, well-dressed Indian man appeared, glancing down at his clipboard. "Frank and Gaye?"

His smile was warm, his eyes welcoming. Gaye knew immediately that this was a person she could trust. Paul motioned them to a pair of couches in his small, inviting office. A set of statues on the coffee table caught Gaye's eye.

"What are these?"

"I'm glad you asked." He picked up the first statue and handed it to her. The heavy stone figure had a simple white front, but a thick black layer blanketed its back, running from the top of its head down. The figure was hunched under the weight of the burden it bore.

"A former client made these," Paul explained. "This one's hunched over, see? That's his burden, shame."

Gaye nodded, feeling the weight of the figure's pose. "I know how that feels."

Paul reached for the second statue. It was the same figure, but now the dark covering was only halfway down its back. It was straighter, the head lifted.

"This is that same person. He's on his way to healing." Paul placed it back and gestured to the final statue. Bright white, this figure stood tall, its face open, free. The shame was gone.

Gaye stared at the third figure, her heart filled with longing. "That's how I want to feel."

"This is the process I take people through," Paul said quietly. "The black weight on the first statue is shame. We're often hunched over from it, right? But I help people find freedom and point them to God. He removes the shame, layer by layer, so they can stand tall again."

Frank pointed to the first statue. "That's both of us right now."

"Then that's where we'll start." Paul nodded thoughtfully. "It doesn't happen overnight. This is a process. You cannot be free of your burden without walking through the process of healing. The way out is through."

The way out is through? Something in that phrase caught Gaye's attention, and when she looked at Frank, she could tell it had spoken to him too.

On the other side of the coffee table, three candles sat in simple holders. He took out a lighter, igniting each one as he spoke. "These represent the Father, the Son, and the Holy Spirit. Everything we do here, we do with God as our guide. Every issue we confront, every emotion we feel, we'll walk through it with Him by our side. The only way out of the darkness is to walk through it, but you will never be alone as you go. God is with you; follow His lead and you will make it through." He leaned back in his chair, letting the candlelight cast a warm glow across the room.

When he sat forward again, he began to tell his own story. His mother was Indian, and his father was American. He talked briefly about his relationship with his dad and how he'd come to work in marriage counseling. His words were soft, his manner calming. A steady spirit filled the room, setting both Frank and Gaye at ease.

"What about you two?" he asked. "What's your story?"

They poured out their years of hurt, anger, and infidelity. They reported Frank's healing from smoking and drinking, but admitted that their struggles with one another continued. Paul nodded occasionally, jotting down a few notes. Then he looked up.

"How long ago was it, Gaye, that you went upstairs and confronted Frank about his adultery?"

"Umm." She had to think. "It's been ten years, at least."

"Since then, how many marriage books have you read?"

She hesitated, unsure how to count. "Dozens, probably."

"How many marriage conferences?"

She shrugged, a wary smile crossing her face. "A lot."

Paul eyes twinkled. "Oh, so I'm not the first counselor you've seen, am I?"

Frank and Gaye broke into laughter. "Not even close."

Paul moved to a stereo system on the side table and turned it on. Soft worship music filled the room. He resumed his seat and closed his eyes, lifting his face slightly. Frank's eyes drifted closed as well.

Cautiously at first, Gaye let herself relax, then she sank into the stillness, lifting her heart in prayer. God's presence settled around her, familiar and comforting. She thanked Him for His faithfulness in not letting them go even through the mess of their lives.

When the music faded, she opened her eyes. Frank was still in quiet worship. She glanced at Paul, who gave them both a moment to stay there.

Finally, he moved to a whiteboard set up beside his chair, picked up a marker, and turned to Frank. "We're going to go into your family of origin now."

"Okay." Frank nodded.

"Frank," Paul said. "Do you remember your grandpa?"

Frank shifted, thinking back. "My grandparents lived in Saint Paul. They passed when I was a teenager. But yeah, I remember them."

"Good. Let's start with your dad's dad. What was he like?"

"Oh boy," Frank said. He recounted what he could, sharing bits and pieces of family lore.

Paul continued, asking about Frank's dad, mom, aunts, and uncles. As Frank spoke, Paul added names and details to the board, drawing lines and jotting down words: *drunk, womanizer, abuser.* His questions kept coming, tracing a complex web through Frank's extended family. Names, relationships, traits, and patterns filled the board in a rainbow of ink.

Gaye watched as the board became a map of pain. For the first time, she was able to see how so many of their patterns of dysfunction had trickled down from their families to them. She sank lower into the couch, the weight of their shared past pressing in.

After two hours, Paul put down his marker. "We'll stop here for today," he said, glancing from one to the other and offering a reassuring smile.

As Frank and Gaye walked past the fountain toward their car, a sense of heaviness accompanied them. The five-hour drive home loomed ahead, filled with swirling thoughts and unresolved problems that blurred together like a turbulent storm.

Two weeks later, they returned for their next session. Paul began their time together by praying for them, and as he did, Gaye and Frank felt a profound sense of God's presence. In that sacred space, they expected to hear from God. Paul's prayers, his calm demeanor, and the carefully chosen music created an environment rich with spiritual warmth.

Paul gathered more information about their families of origin. As Gaye spoke about her father, Paul subtly switched the music to a soft melody celebrating the love of a father. When she recounted her experiences of abuse, soothing tunes about comfort and healing filled the air. The music swelled and softened in tandem with the unfolding emotions in the room, and the lights dimmed to enhance the atmosphere of healing.

Paul listened intently as they shared their stories, laughing when appropriate and asking probing questions. The whiteboard in the corner of the room filled rapidly with names and problems. After two hours of exploration, their family history lay bare, exposing every sin and pain imaginable. The words on the board weighed heavily, like an anchor dragging them deep into despair.

Paul turned to Frank, his expression serious. "Frank, what do you see here?"

Frank's voice was flat. "It looks like puke."

Paul nodded knowingly. "That's your background, your heritage. You were raised in a culture of addictions and alcoholism, steeped in dysfunction. It's your social DNA."

Frank shrugged. "Puke."

With a sweeping gesture, Paul continued. "There's also a spiritual realm. The things you're exposed to in the natural have spiritual consequences. Both of you have been hurt emotionally. All this mess on the board shows it. The wounds run deep."

"I'm ready to do whatever it takes to get through this," Frank declared.

Gaye echoed his sentiment with fervor, her resolve bolstering Frank's.

Paul looked thoughtful yet serious. "The process of healing will take time, but remember—you only get free by walking through the pain." He glanced at his watch. "Our time is up for today."

Frank's frustration bubbled over. "You've gotta be kidding!"

A thick haze of emotions clouded their minds as they drove home. They felt the weight of the process. They knew it had begun, but it seemed to stall each time they journeyed to Minneapolis, leaving them grappling with uncertainty and the yearning for true healing.

The next day, Frank picked up the phone and dialed Paul's number, anxiety tightening his chest.

"Hey, Frank, is everything okay?" Paul's voice was calm, steady.

"Yeah, we're fine," Frank replied, trying to mask the urgency in his tone. "But every time we start getting into things, it's time to leave. At this rate it's going to take us seventeen years to make any real progress. I don't know how to do this, but we need to be there longer."

Paul paused for a moment. "Let me pray about it, and I'll call you back."

Paul called Frank again a couple of days later. "Frank, I'm amazed by you guys. Most people your age will ride it out with a bad marriage or throw in the towel and get divorced. They aren't willing to go through the process of fixing themselves. But I'm astounded by your eager willingness to do the work required to save your marriage."

"Thank you. Yes, we are," Frank said.

"I've never done this before, but here's what I propose," Paul continued. "If you two come up Thursday night, I'll give you from eight a.m. to eight p.m. on Friday and Saturday, and from eight a.m. until noon on Sunday."

"Thank you," Frank said. "We could cover a lot of ground in one chunk of time."

"With your tenacity, I think it would be beneficial," Paul affirmed.

"How much will that cost?" Frank asked.

"Seven thousand for the weekend."

Frank felt a moment of sticker shock but quickly composed himself. "Sounds good. Let me talk with Gaye, and I'll get back to you."

He hung up and turned to Gaye, excitement tempered by the reality of the situation. "This is going to be expensive."

Gaye looked at him. "Our marriage is worth it."

Frank said, "I don't care how much it costs."

A few weeks later, after Frank finished work on Thursday night, they made the familiar five-hour drive to Minneapolis. Feeling hopeful, they settled into a hotel for the night. before entering Paul's office the next day. In the waiting room, a middle-aged woman sat quietly, her hands folded in her lap.

Paul greeted them with warmth, his presence immediately filling the room with a sense of calm. "I want to bathe this process in prayer," he said as he led them into his office. "I pray when we start and we'll continue to speak with God throughout, but I'd like an intercessor prayer warrior with us, too. Would that be okay?"

Gaye glanced at Frank and then back at Paul. "Is that the lady we saw in the waiting room?"

Paul nodded. "Yes, that's Marsha."

Gaye smiled. "The more prayer, the better."

Paul brought Marsha into the room. After a brief introduction, she settled quietly in the corner of the couch. Throughout the weekend, she remained there, praying silently unless Paul directed a question her way.

Paul turned his attention back to Frank and Gaye. "We've covered your family of origin. Now, do you want to be healed?"

"Yes," Gaye replied.

Paul shifted his focus to Frank. "You too?"

"Absolutely," Frank said eagerly.

Paul opened his Bible. "The book of James, chapter five and verses fourteen and fifteen, says, 'Are any of you sick? You should call for the elders of the church to come and pray over you, anointing you with oil in the name of the Lord. Such a prayer offered in faith will heal the sick, and the Lord will make you well. And if you have committed any sins, you will be forgiven.'"

Paul continued to explain the significance of anointing with oil, sharing passages from the Old Testament and emphasizing the spiritual importance of the act. He closed his Bible and met their eyes. "We still use oil today. Something spiritual happens when we do what the Bible says."

Frank and Gaye nodded.

"May I anoint you with oil? I'll pray, and God will bring the healing," Paul asked, his voice filled with compassion.

"Yes," they both said in unison.

Paul opened a small bottle of oil, and the subtle, unique scent filled the space with a sense of sacredness. He placed a drop on his finger and traced the sign of the cross on Gaye's forehead, saying, "In the name of the Father, Son, and Holy Spirit, I anoint you for healing with this oil."

He then turned to Frank, repeating the same gesture. "In the name of the Father, Son, and Holy Spirit, I anoint you for healing with this oil."

At that moment, a deep sense of peace wrapped itself around them. Warmth spread through Gaye as she realized that whatever Paul prayed for would happen. This would be good, no matter what lay ahead.

Paul directed Frank to sit on one couch while Gaye settled next to Marsha on the other. He began with an air of authority, "I will lay down some ground rules. When we enter the presence of God, He may lead one of us to a deep spiritual place. From the outside, it might appear that the other person is uncomfortable or even in pain. This instinct might urge you to offer comforting words or a hug, but don't interfere. Trust God. Allow Him to do the healing. Remain silent. Do not touch. Your role, instead, is to join Marsha in intercessory prayer, asking God to fulfill His plans. It may take time, so be patient. Let the Lord continue His work. If you intervene, it will distract from the process, and you'll risk missing everything God has in store for you."

Gaye glanced at Frank, her eyes wide with apprehension and anticipation.

"Gaye," Paul said, turning his focus to her. "You want to worship God, don't you?"

"Yes," she replied. "But right now, when I'm trying to worship, I can't see His face. I don't feel close to Him."

Paul nodded thoughtfully. "I'm going to give you something." He strode to his desk and returned with a small crucifix about the size of his hand.

Paul placed the cross in her left hand, "I want you to understand, Jesus is no longer on that cross. That's not the purpose of showing you this. But, when Jesus hung there, He was dying for your sins, bringing your salvation."

Gaye looked down at the cross, feeling its weight in her palm.

"Now, put your hand on Jesus and confess your sin."

Paul turned up the music, filling the room with soft melodies, and closed the blinds. The only light came from the warm glow of those three flickering candles. Trusting Paul, Gaye sensed this was a necessary act, even if she didn't fully understand it. She placed her right hand on the crucifix and took a deep breath. "God, I'm sorry. Please forgive me for the sexual sin I committed."

As she spoke, she felt the weight of her sin leave her, as if it were physically transferring onto the cross. A wave of emotion surged within her, and she cried freely, the tears flowing without restraint. After several minutes, as the sobs began to subside, memories of her past rose before her. They were painful, but she recognized them as part of her journey. She had been sexually sinned against, and she had sinned herself as well. In that moment, she turned to Jesus and asked Him to take away the shame, the guilt, and the pain. With every confession, the burden lifted, landing on Jesus on the cross. He didn't ask for anything in return. He simply washed her clean, making her "white as snow."

Tears continued to flow, but now they were tears of relief, healing, and beauty. A sense of peace Gaye had never known enveloped her, a beautiful release from her past.

Frank remained on his couch, a silent witness to the moment unfolding. Gaye sat in a space filled with the weight of her burdens and the presence of God. No one interrupted her as she poured out a lifetime of pain, guilt, shame, and sin. Each drop of sorrow flowed to Jesus on that cross.

She perched on the edge of the sofa, the release raw and cathartic. The torrent slowed, and she regained control over the maelstrom of emotions within. Then another wave struck, fueled by the overwhelming embrace of forgiveness as Jesus revealed how He had been with her even during the darkest moments of abuse and pain. In that sacred space, Gaye leaned back against Marsha, who was sitting quietly beside her. In that moment, in Gaye's heart and mind, Marsha transformed into Jesus.

Her precious Lord embraced her, tenderly rubbing her hair and patting her cheek, pouring out His love like a warm blanket over her weary soul. The sensation was exquisite, unlike anything she had felt before.

Jesus whispered, "You are free. You are clean. You are clear. You are perfect. No more shame, no more guilt, no longer a victim. You are My perfect child."

Tears flowed freely as she basked in His words. "It's finished. You are free."

Taking a deep breath, Gaye moved to sit on the floor in front of the couch. Processing the profound shift within her, she glanced at Frank and felt an immense surge of forgiveness and love for him, the depth of which she had never experienced before.

Eventually, Paul pressed a button on the stereo, and the worship music faded into the background. "How are you doing?"

"I have lived as a victim for fifty-five years." Her voice was full of emotion.

"And now?"

"I don't know. I feel like the gap between God and me is gone. I can feel everything He wants me to feel." She pointed at the burdened statue on the coffee table. "I'm free from all that black stuff."

Paul nodded. "The shame is gone."

"Yes! All the black has been completely wiped away." She gestured toward the third statue. "I'm like him. Upright. Weightless. White before the throne of God. Without shame."

As Gaye received her healing, Frank sat on the couch, lost in prayer. In those moments, God broke his heart for Gaye. A profound sorrow for the pain he had caused his beloved wife filled him, and he realized how much of her suffering stemmed from his own sinful actions and choices. Then a deeper awareness washed over him, a painful realization of how his behavior had also grieved God. He, Frank, had hurt God's daughter, and the weight of that knowledge was almost unbearable.

And God whispered to Gaye, "Give the cross to Frank."

Reverently, she placed the precious crucifix in her husband's hand, passing on the weight of their shared journey, a symbol of her newfound freedom.

Frank stared at it, feeling the enormity of the moment. Paul turned up the music again, and guided Frank gently. "Put your hand on Jesus and confess your sin."

With a deep breath, Frank obeyed. As he placed his hand over the cross, the same cleansing that had washed over Gaye flooded his being.

God moved within him, bringing forth waves of healing. Emotions surged, intense and overwhelming, threatening to explode from within. Just as he thought he might drown in the tide, a moment of breath caught him, a fleeting pause before the next wave of realization.

Frank sensed Jesus standing beside him in that sacred space, and his emotions ignited once more. The healing process unfolded like a symphony, the rich and layered notes resonating deep within his spirit. Time lost all meaning as he surrendered to the flood of feelings.

The quiet closing of a door registered as Paul and Marsha left the room, leaving Frank and Gaye alone in their raw, unfiltered grief. Frank moved beside her on the floor, and they embraced, rocking back and forth, tears flowing freely as they held each other tightly. It was a moment unlike any they had ever experienced, an unbelievable depth of connection forged through shared pain and healing. In this newfound closeness, God granted them supernatural forgiveness for one another, a bond now strengthened by the trials they had faced together.

Frank looked at Gaye and felt a love for her that transcended anything he had ever imagined. Gaye looked at Frank and felt unhindered forgiveness and love. All the pain that they had caused each other was gone.

In time, Paul returned and suggested, "Why don't the two of you relax by the fountain?"

The couple headed down and settled beside the soothing waters.

Gaye said, "I see love coming out of that fountain, washing over and covering us. God has taken my dirty shame and washed me white as snow."

As they enjoyed the moment, a voice pierced through Frank's thoughts: *Frank, you never proposed to your wife.* The realization hit that he hadn't knelt or performed any of the classic romantic gestures. He turned to Gaye, his heart racing. "Will you marry me?"

Gaye laughed, lifting her wedding ring.

"I know, but I want you to have the wedding you never had, the wedding of your dreams. And I want to take you on a honeymoon. Anywhere in the world, wherever you want."

Gaye understood. They both felt it. They agreed they would renew their vows in a special ceremony on August 7, 1999.

Eventually, Frank offered Gaye his hand, and they strolled back to Paul's office, sitting side by side on the couch once again.

Paul opened his Bible with a smile. "God gave me a scripture for you. I'm going to read Ezekiel 36:25–27 from the New Living Translation." His voice resonated with authority as he read:

> Then I will sprinkle clean water on you, and you will be clean. Your filth will be washed away, and you will no longer worship idols. And I will give you a new heart and I will put a new spirit in you. I will take out your stony, stubborn heart and give you a tender, responsive heart. And I will put my Spirit in you so that you will follow my decrees and be careful to obey my regulations.

He handed them a card with the reference on it.

"Thank you," Frank said. "Gaye and I are gonna renew our vows." Paul chuckled in delight.

Frank shared the story of their wedding and the inspiration that had struck him by the fountain. In an unexpected burst of energy, Paul leaped to his feet. "Let's go look for wedding dresses!" He grabbed his car keys and grinned. "Come on, I know the perfect place. I'll drive."

They climbed into his car, excitement buzzing in the air as he navigated to a quaint little shop. Just as they opened the door, a lady in black prepared to leave for the day. She paused, her purse in hand. "I'm sorry, we're just closing. Please come back another time."

But a young woman appeared behind her, smiling brightly. "No, come on in! I'll show you around."

As they stepped inside, Frank's eyes widened at the sight of white wedding dresses lining the walls. Gaye followed the young lady to the back to try on dresses while Frank remained in front with Paul.

"Remember," Paul instructed, "when she comes out, it doesn't matter what the dress looks like simply say, 'You look great, honey. I love it.'"

"No problem," Frank assured him.

Time slipped by. Gaye emerged wearing a stunning white dress. She twirled, radiating beauty and confidence.

Frank didn't need encouragement to tell her how beautiful she was, and Gaye glowed.

"What do you see, Frank," Paul asked.

Frank hesitated. "Do you want me to be honest?" Gaye's eyes widened, but Frank smiled as he examined her closely. Finally, he said, "Her posture has changed."

Paul's eyes sparkled with realization. "You're right. Her shame is gone. This has changed you physically, Gaye."

They didn't purchase a dress that day, but the experience laid an excellent foundation for their restoration process. Paul drove them back to their car and waved goodbye with a smile.

The couple savored a wonderful evening together, their spirits high. After a fulfilling dinner, they returned to the hotel, feeling spiritually exhausted but hopeful.

From this pinnacle of joy, they could not have known that the next day would bring everything crashing down once more.

CHAPTER ELEVEN

Deeper

Frank and Gaye returned to Paul's office the next day. As they took their seats, Paul filled the room with uplifting music, initiating a time of worship. Gaye swayed gently, her hands lifted high in praise, her face lit with joy. Paul sank to his knees, eyes closed, lost in devotion. Marsha sat quietly in a corner with her eyes closed.

But Frank struggled to join in. Though he sang along with the music, something was different. He couldn't articulate the emptiness he was feeling within. With his eyes shut tight and hands raised, he attempted to connect from his heart, but it was as if the melodies drifted by without meaning or engagement. Each song felt distant, void of emotion.

Paul sensed the shift in the atmosphere. He turned off the music and took stock of the room. Gaye wore a radiant smile, but concern etched his face when he glanced at Frank. "Frank, how are we doing?"

Frank shook his head in frustration. "I don't know."

"Something's going on. What are you feeling?" Paul pressed.

"I'm trying to worship but can't connect with the Lord," Frank admitted.

Paul turned to Gaye. "Would you mind going down by the fountain for a while?"

A furrow crossed her brow, but she rose silently and exited the room.

Paul focused back on Frank. "In my experience, when a man can't connect with the Lord, sexual sins often create a barrier. Is there any other sexual sin from your past that you haven't confessed?"

"No."

The intensity in Paul's gaze prompted a moment of silence.

Frank's mind raced back to the one-night stand with Shelly and the time his old girlfriend returned to town. Two brief encounters, each devoid of emotional connection. They felt trivial to him. After years of marriage, how could these two nights matter at all? He recounted both experiences to Paul.

Paul's expression became grim.

"What's wrong?" Frank asked.

Paul shook his head. "Frank, what you just told me is going to crush Gaye."

Frank's mouth went dry.

"This is a sin of omission," Paul stated.

Frank had never considered it in that light.

"You'll have to confess this to her when she comes back."

He shrugged. "Okay, no problem."

"Yes, there is a problem. She's got every right to walk out the door, to leave and divorce you today. This sin is a legitimate reason for divorce."

The air thickened. "What?"

"And I'm not going to say she won't do it," Paul said. "This is going to crush her."

Frank's heart raced. Yesterday had felt so promising, so filled with hope. Were they about to lose everything they had just begun to rebuild? The moments stretched painfully as he waited for Gaye's return.

When she finally entered, Paul remained silent, simply gesturing for Frank to take the lead. Frank felt as if he were standing on the edge of a precipice. He took her hands.

"Gaye, I need to confess something to you. Please forgive me." Gathering his courage, he began to recount the two one-night stands. Each word was a dagger cutting deep. The moment the truth left his lips, hurt washed over Gaye's face. Her eyes filled with tears, her body tense and upright as she absorbed the weight of his confession. Frank's own tears began to fall. The fear of losing his wife consumed him with an unbearable tension.

The revelation struck Gaye like a physical blow. Nausea twisted her stomach. A deep ache settled in her chest. She couldn't have felt worse if he had plunged a knife into her heart. She pulled away, unable to look at him, unwilling to touch him. Betrayal cut through the fabric of their relationship, leaving gaping wounds in its wake.

For twenty long minutes, she sobbed, the tears pouring out as a mix of hurt and confusion. Yet, in the midst of her despair, she felt the comforting embrace of Jesus, holding her close, offering solace in her darkest moment.

Then, as if the world had paused, God spoke to Gaye with a clarity that pierced through her anguish. *"Forgive him."*

It wasn't a thought born from duty or logic or scripture. It was simply a command from God's loving heart. No mental lists of sermons or debates about forgiveness were swirling in her mind. Just the simple, profound call to forgive, accompanied by a supernatural strength that washed over her.

Turning to Frank, Gaye found her voice. "I forgive you, Frank."

As she spoke, joy flooded her heart, replacing the pain and betrayal. She loved him even more than before, a love renewed by grace.

Frank grasped her hands tightly. "You know it all now. It's all out there. No more secrets."

In the light of Jesus's forgiveness, Gaye found the power to embrace her own. She forgave Frank completely and wholeheartedly, releasing the weight of his past and stepping into a future filled with hope.

After the emotional rollercoaster came to a peaceful end, Frank and Gaye began to discuss what their second wedding would look like. They decided to call it their renewal and planned to hold the ceremony in their own home. They called their kids to break the news, and each one responded with cheers of delight. Frank and Gaye's wedding party would include their children, their spouses, and a few close friends.

They wasted no time meeting with a caterer and selecting a mouthwatering menu. Gaye crafted vibrant fuchsia and purple invitations, each adorned with a delicate white dove. With the support of her children, she navigated every step of the planning process. The experience felt exhilarating, as if she were twenty years old again, dreaming and planning for the happy wedding she'd never had.

One day, Frank asked, "Since we didn't get that dress in Minneapolis, what do you want to do?"

Gaye clapped her hands in excitement. "Let's go shopping!"

He drove her to a bridal shop. "Do you have a style in mind? Is there something specific you're looking for?"

Ever since she was a young girl, Gaye had adored butterflies. In their basement hung a beautiful photo of a butterfly emerging from its cocoon, a symbol of metamorphosis and new life. But she didn't have anything specific in mind for her dress.

"I don't think so. I'll know it when I see it." She grinned at him. "You have to stay out here. You can't see it ahead of time."

Gaye felt like a princess twirling in front of the mirrors, but none of the gowns felt right. They went to a few more shops, but nothing caught her attention. Finally, dressed in yet another long, flowing gown, Gaye stepped onto the platform and looked into the multiple mirrors surrounding her. Just then, a whisper from God reached her heart:

"This dress isn't for you, daughter. None of these dresses are for you. They are dirty. You're not dirty anymore. You're pure and white. You need a white wedding dress that no one else has ever tried on."

A shiver of goosebumps cascaded down her spine as God's presence surrounded her. She knew God was for her and felt His love saturate her.

Leaving the store empty-handed, she went home to browse bridal magazines. A magazine from a shop in Chicago caught her eye, featuring a dress that jumped off the page. Gaye fell in love at first sight. The picture didn't reveal every detail, but she felt in her heart that this dress was destined to be hers.

Without hesitation, she called the store in Chicago and spoke to a lady with a heavy French accent. Gaye relayed the style number of the dress. "Do you have it?"

The woman replied, "I was just about to put it on a mannequin in the window."

Gaye couldn't hold back. "Don't! That dress is mine. Wrap it up and put it in the mail." She didn't even ask what size it was. She knew it belonged to her. They paid the $700, and the anticipation grew as she anxiously awaited the arrival of her precious, pure white dress.

When the box arrived, she opened it with trembling hands. As she pulled back the wrapping paper, a stunning gown adorned with embroidered butterflies emerged—symbols of new life that she hadn't noticed in the magazine photo.

The dress fit perfectly. It was absolutely spot-on, and Gaye knew it was a gift from her Abba Father, who had chosen her and loved her deeply. He wanted the best for her. Warmth enveloped her, a divine embrace. At that moment, she felt incredibly loved by God and by Frank.

Their wedding party purchased dresses and arranged the bridesmaids' flowers. Gaye chose fuchsia and purple floral arrangements that captured her contemporary style. The florist crafted stunning centerpieces and selected an abundance of flowers for their backyard ceremony.

On the day of the renewal ceremony, despite pouring rain, Gaye's spirits soared. Their outdoor plans shifted, and the florist transformed their living room into a breathtaking space, creating a focal point around the large windows overlooking the woods. While Gaye prepared at a neighbor's house, family and friends rearranged furniture to accommodate the service and reception indoors.

With guests seated and beautiful music playing, the groomsmen escorted their wives down the aisle. Frank took his place of honor next to the pastor, his heart racing with love and excitement. Their son, Scott, approached Gaye and extended his left elbow, a broad smile lighting his face. She shifted her beautiful bouquet to her left hand, took his arm, and walked down the aisle to meet Frank.

When it was time to exchange rings, their one-and-a-half-year-old grandson, Ethan, stood ready. Clad in a white shirt, little shorts, and suspenders, he held a pillow, waiting for his grandma's cue. When she motioned for him to come, he skipped down the aisle, delivering brand-new rings to Frank with a wide grin, fully embracing his moment in the spotlight.

The ceremony unfolded beautifully as they rededicated their lives to one another in the presence of God and their community. Special friends bestowed memorable gifts upon them including a unique picture featuring all the alphabet letters crafted from butterfly wings. Frank proudly hung the picture on their wall, a constant reminder of hope and rebirth. Paul Sing hand-wrote blessings for each of them on personalized scrolls, further sealing the day's significance and the love surrounding their renewed commitment.

For their honeymoon, Gaye wanted to go to Lake Kabetogama in northern Minnesota. Frank had raved about this unique body of water in Voyageurs National Park for years, recounting his fishing trips with friends. "Gaye, you've gotta see this place. It's just so beautiful."

Having never fished before, Gaye pictured a tranquil cottage by the lake, free of distractions. A place for just the two of them to read and float on the water. Before their ceremony, Frank took her to the backyard and introduced her to a fishing pole. "This is a Zebco closed-face reel with an eight-pound test line."

She feigned interest, listening while he demonstrated how to cast. She practiced throwing a lead weight from one end of the yard to the other. On their first day at the lake, they rented a sixteen-foot boat with a fifteen-horsepower motor and cruised around the calm waters. Gaye sat with Frank, engrossed in her book, as deer wandered nearby and a beaver glided along the shore. The chilly water held no allure for her, and she had no intention of dropping a line.

Frank cut the engine around four o'clock, a couple of miles from the Ellsworth Rock Gardens. He handed her a pole. "You see that big rock over there, with the weeds next to it?"

Gaye peered into the crystal-clear water, spotting smooth rocks twenty feet down and water lilies near a massive boulder. "I see it."

"Cast your line in that direction."

Gaye examined the shiny lure. "Why would anything be attracted to this?" Still, she cast the line with a flick of her wrist, just as she had practiced in the backyard. To her astonishment, a northern pike erupted from the depths and snatched the lure.

"Frank, Frank, he took it!" She began reeling. "Grab the net!"

"It's in my hand, honey!" Frank quickly scooped up her first catch and extracted the hook from the fish's mouth. "Be careful of his sharp teeth and spines," he cautioned as he handed her the fish, which squirmed in her grasp before she released it back into the lake. She quickly picked up her pole for another cast as it swam away.

Gaye was hooked.

Frank navigated them from spot to spot, and they caught fish everywhere they went. Some they let swim free, while others they kept for dinner. As the sun dipped below the horizon, Frank said, "Time to head in."

"Just one more cast," Gaye insisted, flicking her lure back into the water.

Finally, he started the engine, heading back while she reeled in her line. If he hadn't, she might still be out there.

Their long-ago attempt at golf together had flopped, but fishing brought them joy. It was a shared passion, a gift from God, nurturing their bond.

CHAPTER TWELVE

Healing

Though they had made tremendous progress, Frank and Gaye knew God had something more in store for them. They couldn't put it in words, but more healing lay ahead, so they hopped in the car for another long weekend with Paul. The autumn landscape stretched out around them in a symphony of red, orange, and yellow. Bluff-top roads offered sweeping views over the Mississippi River, cast in a warm glow beneath the vibrant canopy. As they descended into Guttenberg, Iowa, a bald eagle soared across the highway two hundred yards ahead, wings spread wide against the open sky.

Stunning.

They passed quaint cottages and farmhouses, each scene more charming than the last. Just as they began the climb up the north bluff, another eagle appeared, gliding mere yards in front of their car. Then it pumped its wings into the wind, crossed the road, and disappeared into the distance.

"Wow," Frank whispered. "I feel like those two eagles mean something."

Gaye glanced over. "Really? What?"

"I have no clue."

Paul greeted them with, "Let's see what God has in store for us today." The meeting began with an extended period of worship. Melodies filled the room.

Frank entered worship with his mind attuned to God's presence. Then, without warning, a vivid and unsettling vision unfolded before him. He stood at the edge of a vast black hole. Cold and dark, it gaped below him—a sheer drop so deep he couldn't see the bottom. The void felt alive, and his pulse raced as he stood there, teetering on the brink. The ground beneath him was uncertain as if it might give way at any moment. Fear snaked down his spine.

Paul sensed the shift and lowered the music. "Frank, what do you see?"

With his eyes still closed, Frank described the scene. His vision remained unchanged—a dark chasm stretching into nothingness before him.

Paul's voice was gentle. "Is God telling you anything?"

Frank hesitated. "I . . . I think He wants me to jump into that hole."

Paul waited, allowing the silence to settle. Then he said, "You have a choice to make, Frank. Right now. If God wants you to jump, what will you do?"

Panic flared. Even though it was a vision, the terror felt raw and visceral. Frank's heart pounded. He knew the jump was just an intellectual decision, yet fear gripped him. The abyss stretched below, a void pulling at his courage.

Paul said nothing more.

Then, in the vision, Frank's feet left the ground. He descended, spiraling into the darkness. *Where's the bottom? What's going to happen?*

Then, as if summoned, a cloud rose from the depths and took the shape of an eagle. It caught him, lifting him safely onto its back. He felt secure as the eagle pumped its powerful wings and carried him upward, out of the dark hole and into the light. The vision faded, leaving him steady and at peace. Frank opened his eyes and looked at Gaye, a soft smile forming.

Paul's gaze was steady. "What happened, Frank?"

Frank recounted what happened in the vision. Then he told Paul about the two eagles they'd seen on the drive.

Paul listened thoughtfully and then asked, "Do you have any idea what it means?"

Frank shook his head. "Not a clue."

Through the afternoon, they explored the concept of fear. Frank shared his fears. First the tangible ones like stepladders and heights. Then he listed intangible ones that haunted him. He confessed to having lived a double life, juggling roles to please everyone else while hiding pieces of himself beneath layers of lies. The weight of maintaining that false self, of remembering the lies he'd spun, had been crushing. He feared rejection, afraid that no one would accept him if they saw his true self.

"I was a phony," he admitted quietly.

Paul guided him deeper, helping him unravel his need to be someone he wasn't. Slowly, Frank began to grasp who he was, a child of God. He was honest and reliable. He could be trusted to show up and keep his word.

The weight lifted. The fear slipped away as though it had never belonged to him. By the end of their session, he felt unburdened, as if a million pounds had been peeled from his shoulders.

Afterward, Paul looked at him with a reflective expression. "Frank, I think if you hadn't chosen to jump into that hole, you might have ended up spiritually dead."

Frank nodded, understanding. He was free to become who he was meant to be. The fear that had gripped him for so long had finally let go. He was no longer worried about others' opinions. He was simply himself.

Now he could climb a ladder to the third story of his house. While it would never be something he'd enjoy, his knees no longer rattled in fear. Gaye noticed it, too.

"You even look different," she said, smiling at him.

Frank felt lighter, inside and out.

Frank and Gaye continued their weekend visits to Paul's office and Gaye shared her story with anyone who would listen. God had worked powerfully in her life, and she wanted others to know it too. She told the whole story to her friend Laura, a stunning woman with glossy dark hair and a striking figure who could easily grace the cover of a magazine. She expressed interest in meeting Paul for some spiritual work. Gaye gladly contacted Paul, and he agreed to meet with Laura on a Saturday, so Gaye made the trip with her to Minneapolis to support her friend.

When Paul opened the door and saw Laura, his first words were, "My, you are such a beautiful woman."

The comment hit Gaye unexpectedly, and a pang of insecurity surfaced. She thought, "What does that say about me?" She forced the thought down, keeping her focus on listening and praying as Paul worked with Laura.

On the drive home, she confessed, "Laura, when Paul said you were so beautiful, it hurt me. He's never told me I was beautiful."

Laura glanced over, surprised. "Oh, Gaye, you're beautiful. You're just as beautiful as I am. That's obvious."

Gaye didn't respond, holding her feelings inside.

Still wrestling with the comment the next day, she turned to Frank. "Have you ever told me I was beautiful?"

Frank was quiet for a moment, then admitted, "I don't know. I've always called you cute."

"Everybody calls me cute. Puppies are cute," she replied. "I want to know if you've ever called me beautiful."

Frank had no answer.

That weekend, they were at Eagle Ridge Resort Golf, on a challenging course known as The General. On the fourteenth hole, Gaye opened up to Frank about Paul's compliment to Laura. By the fifteenth hole, she couldn't hold back tears. She felt plain, invisible, and overshadowed. The sting of comparison had settled upon her. When it was her turn to hit the ball, she took a moment to compose herself, then walked over to take her shot.

As she stood over the ball, a gentle, unmistakable, and familiar voice filled her spirit. *"Gaye, you are My beautiful daughter, and that's all that counts."*

The words pierced through her, the same voice she'd recognized so many times before, her Savior. The warmth of His love wrapped around her, and a profound sense of peace washed away every doubt.

Love. Peace. Joy.

Her God had spoken, and He'd called her beautiful. Those words went beyond any compliment she could receive from another person.

She wept there on the course as her Savior's validation sank deeply into her heart.

When she could finally speak, she told Frank what Jesus had said. She no longer needed anyone else's validation. God had called her beautiful. That was enough.

Frank tried to understand the depth of her experience, and after that he told Gaye often that she was beautiful. His words could never carry the same weight as the voice of her Lord, but she did appreciate them.

In reflecting on Paul's comment to Laura, Gaye found a new clarity. Laura could have her beauty in the world's eyes, but Gaye would rather have the words of the Lord. His words had brought her lasting peace and comfort, sometimes even challenging her in unexpected ways. And above all, they reminded her of her true worth, secure in her Savior's love.

Gaye started her days in the quiet of her prayer nook. One morning, after reading a psalm and worshiping, she closed her eyes to enjoy God's presence. Suddenly, a vision unfolded before her. She was back in her childhood home, standing in the back of the house where her father had thrown her slippers into the furnace. Her father had put his faith in Jesus later in life and had long since passed away, but the pain of what he did that day remained as sharp as ever.

She looked around and realized the slippers were not a part of the vision, but the moment was unmistakable. Then she saw Jesus standing next to her, full of compassion. He wrapped His arm around her, drawing her close. Then, with the same tenderness, He reached out and pulled her father in, encircling them both. Gaye remembered her father's transformation when he became a believer.

As Jesus stood between them, a deep sense of peace washed over her, and the weight of forgiveness settled in her heart. In His grace, Jesus had forgiven her father … and if Jesus could forgive him, so could she.

She focused again on the memory of him throwing her slippers into the fire. The pain was still there. She spoke the words aloud, "I forgive you, Dad." Overwhelming love for her father flooded her heart. It was a love unburdened by resentment, the kind of love that brings freedom from painful memories. From that day forward, a new sense of peace and joy accompanied her father's memory.

Despite the significant healing she had received, however, Gaye continued to be haunted by sudden, jarring childhood memories. The man down the street who did unspeakable things to her, the neighbor who insisted on teaching her how to kiss—it all weighed down on her shoulders.

One afternoon, under the steady stream of the shower, she felt the full force of it all. Tears mixed with the water, slipping down her face as she stood, hands pressed against the wall. In anguish, she cried out, "Why did You let those men take advantage of me?"

Then, a vision appeared before her. Jesus Christ sat upon a massive boulder, dressed in white. His head was bowed, His hands covered His face, and His shoulders shook with deep, sorrowful sobs. His grief was palpable, filling the air with a profound sense of shared sorrow and love.

"That isn't what I wanted for you." His voice resonated with compassion and understanding. "I love you. I'm with you."

The pain around her past left as if washed away by the water. Drying off, she felt lighter, as though a dense gray cloud had dissolved. She got dressed, realizing that the familiar weight of pain and humiliation was gone. Reflecting on the men involved in those painful memories, she found herself newly detached, no longer trapped by the emotions that had once held her captive.

Her healing from that wound was complete.

After a long day at work, Gaye returned home to find Frank settled in his chair, watching television with a newspaper sprawled across his lap. He didn't look up or offer a welcoming word. This continued for days, and the silence felt heavier each evening. Without a glance or acknowledgment from Frank, she clenched her fists and headed to the kitchen to prepare dinner, stewing in her frustration. This routine replayed itself every night for three months, and each time her resentment grew.

Of course, she never voiced her feelings—after all, Frank should know by now that she craved recognition. But night after night, her silence and his indifference built an invisible wall between them.

One evening, after she'd cleared the table and Frank had returned to his chair, she decided to retreat to her prayer nook. There she asked God why this anger was so consuming her. One solitary question. Then she waited. In the quiet she worshipped, singing softly to connect with His presence. A vision came into focus. In her mind's eye, she saw a picture frame. In one corner, her parents argued violently, their shouts and anger vividly remembered from her childhood. In the opposite corner of the frame, she saw herself as a little girl, trembling with fear and bracing for the worst.

God spoke gently to her heart: *"You are being ignored."* The connection between her present anger and past trauma clicked into place. Then His voice reassured her, *"But My love is complete. You don't need anything else."*

The vision faded, leaving her with clarity. She realized her need for Frank's acknowledgment stemmed from her unresolved wounds of being overlooked by her parents. Sitting in God's presence, the old pain melted away, replaced by peace. She no longer needed validation from anyone else—Jesus was enough.

Gaye remained in her nook for a long time, understanding God in a new way—His love is complete. That knowledge made all the difference to her. It even changed how she thought of her husband. Frank wasn't perfect; she knew that well. She loved him in spite of his shortcomings. But Gaye didn't need her husband to complete her. All she needed was Jesus.

With a renewed love for her Savior and husband, she bounded downstairs to share this revelation with Frank. Standing before him, she declared with a smile, "I don't need you anymore."

Frank's face paled, his confusion evident. "After everything we've worked on, you're leaving?"

"No, not at all," she replied quickly. "God's revealed something to me tonight. I've idolized you my whole life. I've placed you above my relationship with Him."

Frank's expression softened as he listened. "So many times," he admitted, "I've felt I couldn't make you happy no matter what I did. I guess I always knew I wasn't enough."

She took his hands in hers. "You don't have to worry about that anymore. Jesus makes me complete."

Relief washed over him. "Thank you."

"For what?"

"For taking that pressure off me. I don't make a very good God."

"No, but Jesus does," she affirmed.

The next evening when she came home from work and found Frank in his usual spot, everything was different. The anger that had gripped her for so long was gone, replaced by a sense of peace and acceptance. While other irritations still arose, she felt lighter, freer, and more at peace.

A few months later, while out shopping, Gaye glanced up and froze. Standing before her was the woman whose husband she'd confessed to having an affair with. She hadn't seen her since that painful evening, but there was no escape, no corner to retreat to.

To her surprise, the woman's gaze was warm. "Gaye," she said, an unexpected kindness in her voice. "I'm a Christian now, and I forgive you."

The words struck Gaye like a force. She felt her face crumple as the woman stepped closer, her arms outstretched. They embraced, both crying.

"When you came to my house that night and told me you had an affair with my husband," the woman said, "I couldn't process it."

A holy peace settled around them.

Gaye said, "After that night, what happened?"

"It wasn't easy. My husband's job relocated him. Eventually, we divorced. I'm back in town now."

"Your forgiveness means more than I can say." Gaye's voice trembled. "Who does something like that?"

The woman's smile was gentle and radiant. "Jesus Christ does."

The two women stood together, united by grace, in a little shop unexpectedly transformed into a place of healing and forgiveness.

CHAPTER THIRTEEN

Narcissism

On their next visit to Paul's office, the atmosphere brimmed with reverence as they worshiped, their voices intertwining with the melodies. After a few moments of reflection on their Savior, Paul began with a beautiful prayer, setting a tone of openness and trust. They settled into their usual spots, and Paul took the lead.

"Frank, this next topic is going to be difficult."

Frank shrugged. "I'm up for anything. What's on the menu?"

"We need to talk about narcissism. Do you know what that means?" Paul asked, studying Frank's expression.

Frank offered a blank stare.

"Clinical narcissism, also known as narcissistic personality disorder, is characterized by a pervasive pattern of grandiosity, a need for admiration, and a lack of empathy," Paul explained.

"Okay, but why are we talking about this?" Frank asked curiously.

"Tell me if any of this sounds familiar." Pulling a book from the shelf, Paul glanced at it, then looked up. "Grandiosity is a pervasive pattern of exaggerated self-importance and superiority. A sense of entitlement occurs when individuals believe they deserve special treatment from others without reciprocating. They also need admiration from others to support their self-esteem and inflated sense of self-worth."

Paul glanced at Gaye, who nodded thoughtfully. Then he turned back to Frank. "Is anything registering so far?"

Frank shook his head. "Nope. Should it?"

Paul focused on Frank. "Manipulative behavior, lack of empathy, a sense of superiority, fragile self-esteem, and difficulty in relationships." He paused. "How are we doing now?"

Frank shrugged, still not seeing any relevance to himself or Gaye. For Gaye, however, the words struck a chord deep within her.

Paul tapped his fingers on the book, maintaining a gentle rhythm. He read off another list of narcissistic attributes. Frank remained unmoved, puzzled even, as the concepts felt foreign, disconnected from his perception.

Paul steepled his fingers. "I just covered the twelve major characteristics of a narcissist. You don't see it yet?"

Frank cleared his throat with a hint of frustration. "No! What do you want me to say?"

Paul sighed. "I'll tell you what we're going to do. I'm going to send you back to the hotel with this book and a blank legal pad. Start with the first trait and think of examples in your life where the characteristic might fit. Write down whatever comes to mind."

"You want me to do that with all twelve?" Frank asked.

"Just do the best you can," Paul urged.

Frank sat on the hotel balcony later that day, feet propped on the railing as he flipped through Paul's book. He read about the traits of narcissism and the wreckage they left in people's lives. Yet, nothing resonated, no matter how he tried to connect the descriptions to his own experiences.

An hour later, Paul called. "How's it going?"

Frank wiped a hand down his face, frustration bubbling to the surface. "It's not."

"What do you mean?" Paul asked.

"Paul," Frank said. "I'm looking over all twelve of these. I don't fit any of them."

"Let me talk to Gaye," Paul said.

Frank handed her the phone. A minute later, she hung up. "He wants me to help you with this."

Frank relinquished the book and the legal pad. "All yours."

Gaye dove into the task. She read a line from the book. Then her pen raced across the page as she filled the legal pad with examples. Her thoughts spilled forth like a dam breaking. Each written word was a testament to moments in their lives that Frank had overlooked or dismissed. After a while, Paul called again. Gaye packed up her notes, ready to return to his office.

Upon their arrival, Paul flipped through the pages of Gaye's writing, his eyes wide. "You have a real-life example for every one of the descriptors of narcissism."

Gaye pressed her lips together. "Just sharing real-life stories."

Paul read aloud from her notes. "I don't even bother to ask him to do things for the kids if golf is on the TV because he'll never say yes." He looked at Frank. "Does that sound accurate?"

Frank dismissed the accusation with a wave of his hand. "That's just the way life is."

Paul continued, reading through Gaye's examples one by one, each accusation more profound than the last. They all seemed nonsensical to Frank, who struggled to see the truth in her words. After setting the legal pad down, Paul raised his palms. "So, none of her words resonate with you?"

Frank smiled, shaking his head. "I guess we all look at life through different lenses."

Paul approached the discussion from various angles, employing a range of creative methods to delve into the topic at hand. Eventually, he locked eyes with Frank. "Do you see a connection?"

Frank let out a heavy breath. "This is getting a little repetitive here, don't you think?"

Paul checked his watch. "It's time to break for lunch. Let's shift gears." He placed the legal pad on his desk. "I've got another idea. Can you arrange to bring your children up here for one of your sessions?"

Frank tapped his chin thoughtfully. "That's going to be difficult. They're spread out across different parts of the country, busy with their own families and responsibilities. I'd be surprised if they could come."

Gaye chimed in. "Let's make some phone calls."

After lunch, Paul initiated a new topic, shifting their focus away from narcissism. They had a list of issues to address, so he picked one and dove in for the rest of the weekend.

Three months later, Paul welcomed Gigi, Scott, Ginger, and their spouses to his office. He said, "You three are going to be the primary focus here. You'll be the only ones talking for a while. I'll ask you questions about how your dad's behaviors affected your life. Frank won't say a word. He won't defend what he did or ask questions. He will sit and listen."

The children exchanged wide-eyed glances.

Paul continued, "Gaye won't say a word either. It's just you guys. Not even your spouses. Okay?"

After a brief moment of hesitation, they nodded in agreement.

Paul said, "Let's start with something simple. What's the first thing that comes to mind when you think of your dad? Who would like to go first?"

Frank shifted nervously in his chair, bracing for the words that would follow.

Scott took a deep breath. "Everything was always about Dad. I caddied for him because I wanted to be with him."

"What else?" Paul prompted.

Scott ran a hand through his hair. "Hunting."

Paul prodded further. "Go on."

Scott continued. "Going hunting was the only time I could spend with him. Even when he was home, he wasn't really there unless he needed more iced tea."

Paul tilted his head slightly. "What do you mean?"

Scott gestured with his hand, mimicking the act of shaking a glass. "The little clink of ice against the glass was our command to refill his tea. We were at his beck and call."

Paul nodded. Frank sat quietly, a sense of dread coming over him.

Scott continued to share examples, his voice steady and unwavering. He didn't hold back; each word was a testament to the pain he felt.

Frank squirmed in his seat, unable to respond.

Paul turned to Ginger, sitting to Frank's left. She took a deep breath. "Dad was never there for us. He was always gone with golf, hunting, and fishing. We had no connection with him." Her voice gained momentum as she told story after story about Frank's failures as a father. Like Scott, she didn't pull her punches. Still, this wasn't easy for her.

Frank instinctively reached out, hoping to offer comfort.

"Don't you touch me," Ginger snapped, jumping sideways out of her chair. Her rejection pierced him, a dagger straight through his heart.

Gigi followed suit, sharing her own stories of disappointment and hurt, painting a picture of a father who had been emotionally absent. Scott piled on again, echoing his sister's sentiments. Ginger filed suit against the pain he had caused. None of them held back.

They delivered blow after blow until they had exhausted their words. Frank sat there, feeling like a dishrag, wrung out and lifeless.

Paul brought in lunch. While the rest of them ate, Frank looked at the pain etched in their eyes, the pain he had caused. His precious daughters had endured so much because of him. His son didn't know the love of a father. How could he have been so selfish?

After lunch, they exchanged goodbyes, and the kids headed off. Frank held his head in his hands as Paul reread the definition of narcissism, concluding with "Frank, you have the clinical diagnosis of a narcissist, one hundred percent."

The words hit like a sledgehammer. It was true. Everything had always revolved around him, every decision, every action. His entire life had been consumed with self. He came before God and everything else. What had he done?

Behind his priorities, everything else had been a distant second, including his family. Paul methodically walked him through the damage he had inflicted. They discussed each characteristic of narcissism, his children's stories providing endless ammunition.

"What happened when your mother lied to you?" Paul asked, his voice steady.

Frank closed his eyes. "You mean when I was a kid?"

"Right. Tell me that story again."

Frank hesitated, memories flickering in his mind like old film reels. "She told Dad I'd done something I hadn't. He beat the crap out of me." Frank's voice trembled, recalling the pain of the past.

Paul's gentle tone urged him on. "What happened next?"

"I hid behind the hedge and vowed to make their lives as miserable as possible. I promised I would live life my own way."

"So, your mom's lie and your dad backing her became a wound. The lie you heard was, 'Nobody believes me.' How are we doing so far?"

"That's about right," Frank replied.

Gaye interjected, "Tell him the Taco Bell story."

Frank hung his head.

"What happened at Taco Bell?" Paul prompted.

Gaye recounted their first visit to Taco Bell.

Paul looked at him with compassion. "Why were you so upset?"

"I don't know. I was just tired."

"Your actions were more than just being tired. It also didn't have anything to do with them not having hamburgers, did it?"

Frank's mouth dropped open.

"You accused Gaye of lying to you."

He nodded slowly.

"When you said, 'You lied to me,' that was a trigger, bringing back memories of your mom lying to you when you were a kid."

Frank closed his eyes, the memories washing over him.

"It's a psychological phenomenon called transference. When you have a reaction far greater than what would make sense for the issue at hand, it's transferring an emotion from a long time ago into the present."

Frank sat in silence, grappling with the new understanding.

"In this case, the trigger was you perceiving her as lying to you." He paused, letting the impact sink in. "It spun you out of control."

"I mean, I couldn't handle my emotions."

"Gaye isn't your enemy."

Frank hung his head.

Paul placed a hand on Frank's shoulder. "When your reaction is much bigger than the event, that's how we know we're dealing with transference."

Frank sighed. "Okay, what do we do about it?"

"You endured the shame of your mother's lies that day and made two vows. The first vow was to make their lives as miserable as possible, and the second was to live your own way, right?"

"I've always struggled with the concept of honoring your mother and father. At Dad's funeral, one of his friends came to me and said, 'Your dad was worried about you ever becoming anything.' When he said that, I felt like I had won."

"You lived according to your vows."

Frank shrugged. "I guess I did."

Paul said, "We're going to cancel those two vows you made that day right now, okay?"

Frank sat in a haze of confusion. "How?"

"Repeat after me. Dear God, that day as a child, I vowed to make my parents' lives as miserable as possible. Right now, I cancel that vow."

Frank's heart raced. He repeated Paul's words.

Paul nodded. "Now tell God, 'I also vowed to live my own way. I rebuke that vow.'"

Frank's voice was steadier this time.

"Good." Paul smiled. "Now, I have a question for you."

"Okay."

"Is narcissism God's plan for your life?"

Frank said, "No."

"Is narcissism a sin?"

He paused, contemplating the question. "I've never thought about that." He looked from Paul to Gaye and around the room, searching for clarity. "Yes, it must be."

"Repeat after me. God, I confess I have been living in the sin of narcissism. I repent of this sin."

Frank closed his eyes. He let Paul's words become his confession. He took a few deep breaths, feeling something shift within him. A river of peace began to flow over him, washing away the tension that had gripped him for so long.

Paul and Gaye watched, smiles spreading across their faces.

Paul prayed for him again, and then they took a short break. Frank wished he could somehow reverse the damage he had done, but the pain he'd caused his children lingered in the air. Maybe it always would.

"Frank," Paul said, breaking the silence. "Imagine Gaye wants to do something with you on a Saturday afternoon, and you're watching the Iowa Hawkeyes take on Ohio State."

Frank hung his head, the scenario cut deep. "Oh boy."

Paul continued. "Here's the exercise you need to do. When you're in a situation like that, take a step back and ask, 'God, what's more important—this football game that I'm probably gonna forget tomorrow or doing something with Gaye?'"

Frank nodded, absorbing the advice.

"Then you'll have a decision to make."

"I understand."

Gaye reached for another tissue.

Frank murmured, "I'll have to do this every day."

Paul agreed. "This will be the most difficult struggle of your life."

The struggle remained. There were moments of frustration and plenty of times of celebrating victories no matter how small. As a couple, they decided take the wins wherever they could find them.

CHAPTER FOURTEEN

Taking the Wins

Frank faced the challenge of overcoming a lifetime of narcissism and nurturing a healthy relationship with Gaye head on. He worked daily to put Gaye's needs first. To do this, he maintained a healthy life of prayer and kept open lines of communication with her. Yet, decades of behavior patterns don't change automatically. Along the way, Frank and Gaye learned to see and celebrate small victories.

One day, they were working through stacks of papers spread across their kitchen table, reminiscing and piecing together the sequence of their stories and debating which ones to include in this book. It was slow, deliberate work, weaving their past into a single narrative.

Suddenly, an unrelated memory surfaced, and Frank had an idea he wanted to capture right away.

"Go get a notebook," he directed without thinking.

He caught the faint flicker in Gaye's eyes. For years, she'd handled small tasks like that without question. But this time, Frank noticed the weariness in her expression, a quiet reminder of the patterns he was trying to break.

Realizing his reflexive slip, he stopped her. "Never mind."

He walked over and grabbed the notebook himself. It was a small, conscious step. The work of unwinding years of ingrained habits takes vigilance and effort. But it was a win. Another step forward in the ongoing struggle to leave narcissism behind.

Frank had always seen himself as a fixer who jumped at any practical problem. If a picture fell and the frame cracked, he mended it without a second thought. But when Gaye got sick, things weren't so simple. Frank couldn't fix her. He wanted to care for her but was out of his depth. When she was too ill to cook, he knew it meant he'd be preparing meals. In the past, when Gaye was under the weather, Frank left her to fend for herself. If he was particularly generous, he'd heat up a pot of Lipton's noodle soup (they called it "sick soup") and turn on the TV.

But with the new outlook on his marriage, Frank stepped out of his comfort zone and worked in the kitchen. He made a simple dinner, set the table, and they ate sick soup together. Gaye only sipped at her soup, her appetite dulled by illness, but she appreciated the gesture. After dinner, she stretched out on the couch while Frank cleaned the kitchen, a task he never would have touched before. All this he did without resentment as an act of service to the woman he loved.

Another win.

Gaye had been feeling worn down and feverish for nearly three weeks, wrestling with a persistent bladder infection. She'd been to the doctor multiple times and endured several rounds of antibiotics. Some days were better than others, but she hadn't fully bounced back. At one appointment, the doctor gave her a new medication and took blood cultures.

As Gaye prepared to leave the office, the nurse explained, "The test takes a few days. If the infection has spread to the blood, that's serious. If we give you a call, you must come to the hospital immediately."

As she stepped outside, a wave of anxiety took hold of Gaye. What if the new medication didn't work? What if she needed to go to the hospital? She couldn't go alone. She didn't *want* to go alone.

That evening, they were discussing plans for the upcoming week, when Frank said, "I'm heading into work tomorrow."

Gaye raised her palm. "If I have to go to the hospital, who will take me?"

He shrugged. "I need to go to work."

Gaye's shoulders sank. "Okay. I guess I can take myself to the hospital if it comes to that."

In the morning, she tried to rally enough strength to make herself breakfast, though every step felt like wading through molasses. Frank joined her in the kitchen, busy pulling out bread and cold cuts to pack his lunch.

She looked up. "What are you doing?"

He didn't miss a beat. "Making lunch, getting ready for work."

Gaye steadied herself and looked him in the eye. "I'd really like you to stay home, just in case I need to go to the hospital."

He paused, finally meeting her eyes. "Oh, I didn't know that's what you wanted." Without another word, he put the bread away and called his boss to say he wouldn't be in. It was a small but profound gesture, a win in the ongoing work to understand each other's needs.

A few days later, the blood cultures came back negative, and Gaye's energy improved steadily. Frank's unexpected support had buoyed her spirit.

In the stillness of her prayer nook, Gaye sat with Jesus reflecting on the long journey of her marriage. For decades, Frank had lived a narcissistic life, leaving her and the children alone and filled with resentment. Now, with narcissism in the rearview mirror, he was a changed man. Gaye also saw how deeply ingrained her victim mentality had been. She had been convinced she was powerless to change anything. She had despised Frank, yelled at him, packed up the kids and taken them to hotels. She'd even thrown his clothes out on the lawn, twice. Yet, Frank had remained oblivious. As a narcissist, he'd been unable to hear her and was unaware of her turmoil.

That evening, she approached her husband after dinner with her Bible in hand. "Frank, I want to talk to you about something. I can do it now because narcissism is in your past."

He turned off the TV and looked at her.

"I want to ask for your forgiveness for not speaking up all the times you hurt or ignored me. In doing so, I enabled you in ways that hurt us both."

Frank tilted his head. "What do you mean?"

"I should have been clear with you. I should have asked you to stay home more. To be a father to our children and a husband to me. I didn't know how to ask."

Frank shook his head. "Back then, I don't think I had the capacity to hear you." He rubbed a hand down his face. "I was living my own way, defined by a set of vows I'd made as a kid, and I didn't even know it. Even if your communication was perfect, it still would have been a struggle." He drew her in for a hug. "I forgive you. And I'm sorry too."

After a minute, she opened her Bible to Ephesians 5 and read verse 25 aloud. "'For husbands, this means love your wives, just as Christ loved the church.'" Her voice trailed as she looked up at Frank. "Jesus gave up His life for His church to make her holy and clean. Husbands are called to love like that. Now that you've changed, part of my journey is helping you know what I need."

Her words reached deep. The two of them spent the following moments in quiet reverence, thankful for the grace that had brought them this far.

How would marriages look if husbands loved their wives like Christ loved the church? Husbands and wives would both savor little victories.

Every win is a step closer to the marriage Jesus wants for them.

Despite all the healing they had received, Gaye continued to struggle with panic attacks. Though the victory during the airplane ride was an amazing win, she still struggled. The attacks were unpredictable and debilitating. Pressure closed in from all sides, she couldn't catch her breath. Her heart would race, pounding erratically while dread and terrible fear surged through her. It was as if the very space around her was shrinking, tightening, and leaving her trapped in an overwhelming, choking sensation. Frank did what he could to be understanding and helpful, but the anxiety remained.

When Gigi invited Gaye to Naples for spring break with her daughters, Gaye wanted to go. The trip promised lots of family time and warm beaches, but the thought of traveling weighed heavily on her.

She went to her prayer nook and asked for guidance. God's voice responded, clear and specific: *"You need to go."*

Reassured, she packed her bags, leaning into the adventure with newfound hope. Together, they set off, imagining themselves lounging on white sands under the sun. The trip there was fine, but as they headed toward the beach that first day, a sudden darkness crept over Gaye. The world narrowed around her, stealing the air from her lungs. Her chest pounded with suffocating anxiety.

Finally, she managed to speak. "Gigi, I can't. I'm experiencing such anxiety right now. I don't know what to do."

Without hesitation, Gigi said, "Let me pray for you, Mom," and words of calm and comfort flowed from her. As suddenly as it had come, the anxiety melted away. Gaye's breathing steadied, and her heart calmed. Grateful, they continued on and spent the rest of the day enjoying the peace of the beach.

When she returned home, Gaye told Frank about the trip and the panic attack that seized her. Frank asked, "Do you think your panic attacks have something to do with the time you were shut in the closet when you were a little girl?"

She shook her head slowly, the memory distant and vague. "I don't know. I don't think so. I haven't thought about that in years."

Two days later, in her prayer nook, she sat alone, her mind drifting through memories and devotions. Reading about walking in the light, the sensation of darkness during her recent panic attack came back to her. She closed her journal. "God, does this have something to do with what happened in that closet?"

In an instant, God granted her a vision. She saw herself, small and vulnerable, back in that closet. But this time she was not alone. Jesus was seated beside her, pulling her into His arms, His hand stroking her hair with gentle care. The closet, once a place of shadow, now glowed with light. The darkness was gone—and Gaye realized that Jesus's presence had transformed it; His light had taken away the fear.

As she returned to the present, peace filled her heart, the shame and shadows lifted. God had healed her. She hasn't suffered a single panic attack since that day.

CHAPTER FIFTEEN

Enmeshment

Gretchen had woven herself deeply into Frank and Gaye's life. She had invited herself and her husband on every vacation Frank and Gaye took and insisted on spending Christmas and every holiday with them. In addition, she'd continued dissecting every one of their counseling sessions. They talked for hours about those sessions, and every time Gretchen sensed hesitation or frustration, she'd snap. "Why aren't you doing the work? This won't improve unless you commit."

Though Frank and Gaye made great strides with Paul, Gretchen's grip didn't lessen. The phone rang almost nightly, bringing with it her intense critiques and demands, often leaving Frank and Gaye drained and anxious. The calls were a constant invasion of their marriage.

When Gretchen and Mike visited, their presence came with its own tension. Her insistence on private discussions made family time awkward. One evening, as the family settled in for cards or puzzles, Gretchen and Mike positioned themselves alone on the other side of the room.

The following morning, Gretchen confronted her brother. "How dare you exclude us. We sat like outsiders while you all enjoyed yourselves."

Frank fumbled for a response and offered a quiet apology.

After they left, Gaye shared her exasperation. "I can't handle her anymore. Why does she cling so desperately?"

Frank answered softly. "I'm her only remaining family."

Gaye shook her head. "But what about us? She's driving the rest of us crazy."

Frank sighed, torn between loyalty to his sister and his own marriage. Gaye met his eyes.

"You can't keep sacrificing us to hold on to her approval, Frank. You need to leave and cleave."

Her words struck deep. Frank knew he was at a crossroads but had no idea what to do.

"Remember what Paul always says—the way out of something is through it. Let's ask Paul."

During their next session, Gaye explained the intricacies of their relationship with Gretchen. Paul listened attentively, asking questions as they laid out stories that painted a picture of the complex, tense dynamic.

Paul steepled his fingers. "Gretchen's carrying a deep pain. She needs affirmation. Her drive to counsel others likely stems from her own difficult experiences."

"We need to do something," Gaye said. "We can't go on like this."

Paul nodded. "You are enmeshed with her."

"What does that mean?" Frank asked.

"Enmeshment," Paul clarified, "is a dysfunctional relationship marked by blurred boundaries, over-involvement, and a lack of individual autonomy."

Frank held up a hand. "Enough of the psychobabble. Explain it in English."

Paul grabbed a napkin and drew a small circle on it. "This represents God, Frank, and Gaye." He looked at each of them. "No one else belongs in this space unless they're invited." Then he drew a larger circle around it. "This is where your kids fit. No other people, not work, not ministry."

Frank shifted uncomfortably, sensing where Paul was headed.

Paul added a final outer ring around the circles. "This is the space for extended family, where Gretchen should be. You have allowed her into the innermost circle where only God, Frank, and Gaye should be." He wrote her name in the center. "That creates a problem."

"It's suffocating," Gaye blurted.

"We need to establish boundaries," Paul said. "Remember when you brought your kids here for a session?"

Frank winced, recalling that difficult session. "Oh no."

Paul pressed his lips together. "She's a counselor. If you try to do this on your own, she'll know exactly how to counter you." He looked at them both. "Invite Gretchen and her husband to our next session. Bring your kids too."

A month later, Paul welcomed a large group to his office. Gretchen and Mike joined Frank, Gaye, and their children. Setting the tone immediately, Paul guided Frank and Gaye to seats in the center of the room, then asked their children to form a circle around them. Finally, he turned to Gretchen and Mike.

"Today, your role is as observers." He positioned them outside of the circle and against a wall. "You're here to watch them, to see them as a family unit."

Paul led Frank, Gaye, and their children through a series of exercises, creating a calm and natural flow of communication. Frank glanced over at his sister. Her face reddened as she watched from the outside. Mike reached over to steady her. She brushed his hand away.

After an hour, Paul addressed Gretchen directly. "This family needs their space." He talked about healthy boundaries for a while and what families needed as their own space. Then he concluded, "To set this boundary, you two will not contact Frank and Gaye for six months."

Gretchen looked like she was ready to erupt.

Paul turned to Frank and Gaye. "You are not to reach out to them either."

They both nodded, feeling relief.

Paul ushered Gretchen and Mike out the door, then came back and made some concluding remarks to the rest of the family before dismissing them.

A quiet peace settled into the Grote's home. The absence of nightly calls from Gretchen brought a new sense of calm. Their lives became their own.

On subsequent visits, Paul continued to check in to see if Frank had made contact with his sister, then they went on to deal with other subjects.

At the end of those prescribed six months, Frank realized he was hesitant to reconnect with Gretchen. The weight of calling her was overwhelming. He played out the conversation in his head and heard her condescending remarks. Shaming.

It was too much. He didn't call.

A year after the intervention, when they visited Paul for a scheduled visit, he met them in the lobby. "I have a surprise for you."

Frank and Gaye looked at one another, smiling.

"Gretchen and Mike are here. Would you like to meet with them?"

The smiles disappeared. Frank and Gaye both felt an instant, visceral reaction. They could already sense Gretchen's pent-up anger ready to unload.

Gaye shook her head, clearly uncomfortable, but they followed Paul to a small room and waited. Gretchen entered and immediately launched into a barrage of accusations.

"How dare you! Who do you think you are? How *could* you—" With words sharpened by time and fury, she poured out every grievance she'd harbored, blaming Frank and Gaye for everything in a storm of reproach.

Frank and Gaye took every dagger quietly, without response. Finally, as Gretchen's tirade simmered, Paul looked to Gaye.

"Would you like to respond?"

Gaye hesitated, but with Paul's encouragement, she spoke. In a moderate tone, she detailed the impact of Gretchen's criticisms and the pain of repeated put-downs and guilt. She illustrated her point with one example after the next. Her volume grew as she poured out years of frustration.

Gretchen tried to argue back, yelling in return. The room became a space for releasing decades of pent-up grievances.

Finally, Gaye's voice cut through. She pointed her finger at Gretchen and yelled, "Selfish! That's what you are—selfish, selfish, selfish!"

Silence hovered over the room.

Paul spoke softly to Gretchen. "This was never about you. No more manipulation. No more inserting yourself into Frank and Gaye's business."

His statement hung in the air.

Gretchen stepped back outside of the new boundary.

Mute.

Her demands and years of influence began to recede.

From then on, Gretchen and Mike kept their distance.

Peace settled in for Frank and Gaye. A newfound freedom blossomed. They spent vacations with various friends of their own choosing. They celebrated Christmas and other holidays with their core family. They enjoyed visits to Paul without constant oversight.

Jesus had won over the enmeshment that had plagued them, illuminating the need for boundaries—clear, sturdy lines that preserved the sanctity of family circles. As poet Robert Frost once noted, "Good fences make good neighbors." Those fences serve as essential boundaries in relationships.

CHAPTER SIXTEEN

God Speaks

God communicates in ways as varied as the souls who seek Him. Some people sense His presence in nature's quiet grandeur; others hear Him in a clear voice. For Frank and Gaye, time spent outdoors has been a direct channel to God's messages. Another particularly memorable way was that they often stumbled upon coins during significant life moments, a small, unexpected reminder of God's presence.

One fishing trip to northern Minnesota in early June stands out for both of them. Frank and Gaye had become mired again in deep misunderstanding. Words seemed tangled, falling short as they tried to communicate. Each felt unheard until, frustrated, they decided to break for lunch, boating over to a nearby campsite. As they sat down at the table, they noticed two pennies lying there, seemingly out of context.

Frank picked up the coins and looked at Gaye. "You know what our money says on it?"

Gaye nodded. "In God we trust."

The words struck them both. A simple penny, another reminder of faith. Their conversation softened, their frustrations untangled, and they left the spot feeling renewed, knowing God was guiding them. From then on, money seemed to show up in their lives at random moments, each time providing a subtle reassurance, a quiet nudge that they were on the right path. Finding money was like God's gentle wink, His confirmation to them.

Even during a hard season, God's presence became unmistakable. Their daughter, Gigi, faced a diagnosis of thyroid cancer. Frank and Gaye prayed without ceasing, wrapped in a constant thread of hope and supplication. In church one day, as Gaye prayed, she heard God say, *"I've healed Gigi."* In the parking lot as they left, they found another coin, a sign that made them feel God's promise.

When Gigi emerged from treatment cancer-free, they couldn't help but attribute her healing to divine intervention. Every time they encountered a coin, no matter the amount, they felt a renewed sense of "In God we trust."

This pattern has continued over the years. While they prayed or faced family challenges, they would often find a dime, a quarter, or even a dollar. To others, these coins might seem random, but to Frank and Gaye, they were messages dropped by God Himself. The habit of finding money has become an intimate dialogue between them and the Divine, especially during rough patches when they need to feel God's nearness.

Golf outings, local parks, and shopping trips all became settings for these sacred moments. Frank and Gaye didn't see the money as mere currency. Each coin, each bill, was a message from God. They filled jars with the coins and took them to fundraisers, giving back as a way of returning God's provision.

Through these simple acts of finding, saving, and giving, they continued to hear God say, "I'm here with you." Each small piece of currency was a symbol of trust, faith, and the loving guidance they felt each day.

Frank and Gaye sat together at a small table in Chick-fil-A, finishing lunch, when an old friend walked in. They hadn't seen her since their wild drinking days with that notorious friend group, known for late-night drinks, crossing lines, and indulging in affairs. Those days felt like a distant, different lifetime.

The woman spotted them and stopped at their table. "How are you two doing?"

They exchanged a few minutes of lighthearted small talk before she grew serious. "This is really amazing."

Frank raised an eyebrow. "What's amazing?"

"When we were all hanging out," she said, "everyone thought you two would be the first to get divorced."

Frank and Gaye exchanged a quick glance. Frank shrugged, but Gaye saw the same flicker of memories in his eyes. It had been a hard road, no doubt about it.

Their friend continued, "We all watched you struggle. It was tough on you both. But I got divorced, the others split up, and here you are, still married. How did you do it?"

"We have God to thank for that." A smile crossed Gaye's face. "We learned that the way out is through."

Gaye had a gold cross engraved with "He saves," purchased as a memento to mark the many transformations in her life. It became a deeply personal symbol of faith that she wore proudly. Later, Frank added a small golden Christian fish for her birthday. Gaye had a jeweler mount the fish on the cross, creating a single pendant she wore for years as a constant reminder of God's love and the healing she and Frank had experienced together.

Over time, Gaye misplaced the pendant, but the loss did not sever her need for a symbol of faith and healing. She found a silver cross and a fish charm of similar size and again had a jeweler bond them together. The new pendant became her everyday adornment, a visible testimony to God's redemption in her life.

With a desire to extend her legacy, she had additional copies of the pendant crafted. She gave a pendant to each of her daughters and her daughter-in-law.

Frank and Gaye knew that sharing their story with family was essential to conveying how God's love had reshaped their lives. They also hoped to use their story as a cautionary tale, but this took courage. Their story was laden with painful memories of sins committed, addictions endured, and misunderstandings about God's nature. Still, as each of their grandchildren reached an age of understanding, they invited them on an outing to a local park.

There, sitting around a picnic table. they opened up, sharing the brutal truths of their past and acknowledging the pain their actions had caused. They discussed respect and spoke openly about struggles with sin and addiction. Most importantly, they shared the hope they had found in Jesus, praying together that their grandchildren would grasp the depth of God's love without having to walk the same rocky path.

They assured each one that, should they ever feel hopeless, they would be there to help. Then they gave each grandchild a cross pendant or bracelet like Gaye's as a reminder of God's faithful love.

The Tri-State Pregnancy Center opened in 1994 as a sanctuary for women facing unplanned pregnancies, offering support in times of crisis. As a woman on the other side of her crisis, Gaye felt drawn to help and applied to volunteer. The executive director, Judy Adelman, saw something in Gaye and welcomed her onto the team. Eager to serve, Gaye took on whatever tasks were needed, from keeping the space tidy to observing the work around her. Soon, she was immersed in a daily rhythm of appointments as young women arrived, each with her own set of challenges and fears.

Alongside a team of dedicated volunteers, Gaye performed pregnancy tests, shared the gospel, and led parenting and prenatal health classes. When young women came seeking solace after the emotional toll of an abortion, she gently directed them to a counselor who specialized in post-abortion support.

Every corner of the Center bore evidence of Gaye's thoughtful touch. She painted the rooms in vibrant, inviting colors and organized bins to store clothes and supplies. Gaye felt an unexpected sense of belonging and camaraderie in this place.

After about six months, Judy called Gaye into her office. "You're becoming a mentor to the volunteers," she said. "I see you as our director of client services."

Gaye's mouth hung open in shock. A decade ago, she would never have imagined that a person like her, someone with a past so marked by pain and shame, would be in a position of leadership. But here she was, being offered the responsibility of guiding others through their own moments of crisis. A wave of uncertainty swept over her. Was she ready for this? No. She didn't feel worthy to submit an application to the board for the position.

After months of encouragement from Judy, Gaye reluctantly submitted an application to the board for the new role. Then she promptly went to her prayer nook and asked God for the board to reject her application.

The board accepted her with open arms.

In the years since then, Gaye has met people from all walks of life, individuals whose stories she could not have imagined. One day, a man named Rick entered the Center, his bald head covered in tattoos, including bullet holes etched into his scalp. At first, Gaye hesitated to meet his gaze. But she brought him to her office and sat with him asking, "How can I help you?"

He said, "Can you help me be the best dad I can be for my little daughter?"

Gaye began meeting with Rick regularly and enrolled him in their First Steps program where he learned parenting skills and earned baby supplies. Despite his rough exterior and a history of trouble with the law, Rick was determined to prove he could be a good father. He worked hard, asking thoughtful questions and showing a genuine desire to care for his child.

One of Rick's many challenges was a lack of transportation, so Gaye began delivering the diapers and supplies he had earned directly to his home. She'd pack them in little bundles and add a small red bell to each one, a symbolic reminder of the support he was receiving.

Eventually, Rick found himself in trouble with the law again. He called Gaye from jail and told her about the unusual peace he was feeling—a sense of calm he couldn't explain. Gaye knew immediately what it was. "That's God," she said.

They spent hours talking. Gaye shared the gospel with Rick, walking him through the story of Jesus's love and redemption. When Rick's court date arrived, Gaye spoke to the judge on his behalf. She told him about Rick's efforts to turn his life around. The judge showed mercy and offered leniency.

Just before Christmas that year, however, Rick's life took another painful turn. His child's mother, grappling with her own set of struggles, ran away with their baby. Rick no longer needed the Center, and Gaye lost touch with him.

On Christmas Day, Gaye and Frank returned home from church to find a small Christmas ornament hanging on their front door—a golden netting holding a red bell inside. There was no one around, but Gaye knew immediately who had left it. It was Rick's way of saying thank you.

Gaye spent over a decade at the pregnancy center, walking alongside countless young women and men in crisis and witnessing God's miracles in their lives. But then, in 2004, God began to open new doors for Gaye and Frank, leading them into new avenues of ministry.

CHAPTER SEVENTEEN

The Way Out Is Through

In 2004, a friend invited Gaye to join in prayer with another woman from their church. The woman shared her story, and in return, Gaye revealed her journey. Having walked this path numerous times, Gaye guided her new friend through the process of listening prayer and brought the woman before Jesus. Together, they sat in His presence and listened for His voice.

As they prayed, Jesus took the woman back to the place where her shame had begun. Then Gaye showed her to the root of a lie she had believed. With gentleness, Gaye had the woman rebuke the lie, and Jesus replaced the lie with His truth. The shame dissolved like mist, leaving only God's precious love behind. Gaye facilitated the encounter, but Jesus did the healing.

When Gaye's friend sent more people to her, she set up a schedule to meet with women regularly. People began inviting Frank and Gaye to share their story at small-group Bible studies and other gatherings, and they were happy to do so. They didn't hold back, and they didn't just highlight their victories. They shared their whole ugly, painful journey, and the response was overwhelming. There was no condemnation, only encouragement and support.

Their vulnerability opened doors for others. A few people asked if they could meet with them individually. When they met, Frank and Gaye were keenly aware of the pain these individuals carried. They discerned origins and guided folks to Jesus, who provided healing. As they continued to meet with more people, one after another received profound healing. Abba, their loving God, spoke directly to the lies that had held them captive, replacing them with truth and bringing them into the light of His love.

As the years passed, Frank and Gaye continued to meet with people in need. They spoke in small groups, taught classes at church, and offered one-on-one sessions, all while being witnesses to the transformative power of God's healing. The people who came to them were hurting, broken, and wounded. They were young and old, single, married, divorced, or remarried. Some came seeking something to fix their spouse, others came ready for healing themselves. All of them needed transformation through Jesus.

Frank and Gaye taught people to worship God fully, with heart, mind, and soul. They taught them to recognize their triggers, trace them to their sources, and ask Jesus to reveal the lies that had taken root. And once Jesus revealed those lies, He also brought the truth to replace them. The rest of the healing process was up to God. Frank and Gaye were happy to offer guidance, but they made it known that true healing would only come through time spent with Jesus, through prayer, journaling, and seeking His voice.

One year, they received an email from a young couple named Dennis and Jennifer. The couple had heard about Frank and Gaye through their website and reached out for help. The Grotes invited the couple to their home, where they shared a condensed version of their story, then listened to Jennifer and Dennis, who were both deeply scarred by past abuse. They had fallen into patterns of blaming each other for the issues in their relationship.

Frank and Gaye worshiped with them, listened to Jesus, and walked the couple through the same healing process they had experienced. Over the course of multiple sessions, they worked through one issue at a time, praying and seeking God's truth. As the couple made prayer a regular habit, their hearts began to change. They kept returning and gradually, the transformation became evident.

At the opening of one session, Dennis sat with his head down, embarrassed. "Last night, we got into a horrible fight."

Frank clapped his hands encouragingly. "Great! Tell me about it."

Dennis was stunned. "What do you mean, great? I thought we were making progress."

"Sure," Frank said. "But our fights sometimes reveal the next issue we need to work on."

So Dennis shared his story while Frank and Gaye listened, asking questions and drawing out the details. Then Frank spoke to Dennis with a calm urgency. "Your past is blocking your ability to communicate with your wife. You need to face that and break through it with God's help. Let Him guide you to the hurt in your past that He wants to heal. Once you do that, you'll connect with your wife in a whole new way. You'll be able to communicate in love and intimacy. This is God's work, done by the power of the Holy Spirit."

Dennis nodded.

Frank placed a hand on his shoulder. "The way out is through, my friend."

Over time, Dennis and Jennifer applied the tools Frank and Gaye had shared. Their communication improved, and their marriage found peace. They no longer needed to see Frank and Gaye regularly. They had done the hard work and were living in freedom.

Over the years, Frank and Gaye have continued to listen to Jesus, individually and together. They have heard His voice and have responded to His call. They understand that their healing is not meant to end with them. They have been through the mess and have emerged on the other side. Now they are called to help others do the same, to walk out of their shame and into freedom.

The work is not easy. It requires vulnerability and intentionality. Not everyone choses to engage in the process, and not everyone is willing to put in the hard work. But for those who do, the reward is freedom.

The key is seeking Jesus. God honors every step taken toward Him. The door is ajar. Come as you are.

Whatever difficulty you are facing, the way out is through. With Jesus by your side, you can step out of your darkness and into God's marvelous light.

Contact Frank and Gaye

Frank and Gaye Grote have been called to help others on their journey to healing and wholeness through the light of Christ. They serve broken and hurting individuals, couples, and families who want freedom from emotional pain caused by false beliefs that were instilled during the formative years.

As a child, Frank was sexually, emotionally, and physically abused, which resulted in deep misconceptions about himself and God and led to multiple issues in his adult life. Today, with Jesus's help, Frank has been freed from narcissism, anger, alcoholism, womanizing, and adultery. "Jesus brought me to the end of myself," Frank says, "so I could meet Him there and get to know Him as the Savior He is."

Gaye was a victim of sexual abuse and parental neglect. She carried deep fears, heavy shame, and dreadful guilt. She became an enabler, codependent, and an adulterer. She lived as a victim of her trauma for fifty-five years, but surrender to Christ changed her life. She humbly declares, "Jesus changed my heart and set me free!"

Do you want to be set free?

Contact Frank and Gaye:
Email: intothelight.com@gmail.com
Website: FrankandGaye.com

Acknowledgments

We give all glory to our Lord and Savior, Jesus Christ.

We could never have completed this project without help and encouragement from our beloved family and friends.

To all the precious people who have sat in our home and wanted more, who have spoken the truth in love and, despite their problems, have realized that the way out of their struggles was to go through them with Jesus. We are so proud of you. God bless you all.

Thank you to our spiritual daughter, Brooke Althoff, and her children, Frankie and Charlotte, for their prayers and encouragement throughout the writing of this book.

Our dear friend, Heather Heim, has boosted us in every way, encouraging us to share our story to help other people. Her wonderful husband, Brian, came up with the vision of the light coming through an open door that we have used on the cover.

When we shared our testimony in a small-group setting, someone said the phrase we've heard so many times—"You guys should write a book." Andy DeWitt piped up and said, "I outlined eight chapters while you were talking." This led to him taking the lead in crafting and constructing our story in detail. He's been a joy to work with.

Our Tuesday night community group members have been a source of constant encouragement in our journey. They have prayed for us, walked alongside us, were excited with us, and were incredible. These wonderful people include Abby and Kevin Regan, Sam Scheer, Brittni Webber, Chris and Bethany Herrin, Paul and Kenzie Hallbick, Christian Melton, and Devon Garcia.

Roger and Diane Arensdorf, thank you so much for loving us, staying in touch with us, praying for us, and just being there for us over the years.

Thank you to our special neighbor, Linda Abitz, for always offering a listening ear and encouragement.

Finally, Mark and Martha Hansen always ask how we're doing, they pray for us, and they gave us a gift which means the world to us.

www.ingramcontent.com/pod-product-compliance
Lightning Source LLC
Chambersburg PA
CBHW050905160426
43194CB00011B/2299